Broken Pieces, Shattered Dreams, and Severed Relationships

By

Prophetess Theodoria West

authorHOUSE™

1663 LIBERTY DRIVE, SUITE 200
BLOOMINGTON, INDIANA 47403
(800) 839-8640
WWW.AUTHORHOUSE.COM

First published by AuthorHouse 07/13/05

ISBN: 1-4208-1531-8 (e)
ISBN: 1-4208-1530-X (sc)

Printed in the United States of America
Bloomington, Indiana

This book is printed on acid-free paper.

ACKNOWLEDGMENT

This book is dedicated in loving memory of my late son, John Antonio Clements, 1974-1994, my daughter, Nichole Crawford, my son Canvas Clements and my husband Bobby West, Sr.

I honor my Pastor, Bishop Gus Kilgore, Jr. and Assistant Pastor, Joanne Kilgore, who are also my spiritual parents. I thank them for their encouragement and prayers, as they held me up before the Lord and for allowing me to follow in their footsteps as they follow Christ. I especially honor them for being a real man and woman of God.

The greatest honor and thanks of all I give to our Lord and Savior, Jesus Christ for saving my soul from a burning hell, who paid in full the price for our sins, giving us eternal life. I do honor him with my life and everything that I am and all of my possessions. A good God bless you to my editors Minister Hope Griffin and Darlene Simmemon, who worked so hard to help put this book together. To God be all the glory! And thank you to all of my friends and relatives that supported me in deeds and prayers. May the Lord continue to bless and prosper you, in Jesus Name. And a special thank you to a dear and precious cousin who inspired me to write this book due to his parent's death: James "Baby Brother" McLaughlin. Amen.

Table of Contents

ACKNOWLEDGMENT...v

FORWARD ix

INTRODUCTION xiii

CHAPTER ONE BROKENESS......................................1

CHAPTER TWO FRIENDLY FIRE 9

CHAPTER THREE HOW DO YOU PATCH THE TITANIC? 17

CHAPTER FOUR STAND FIRM IN YOUR FAITH 25

CHAPTER FIVE STAND, PRESS AND FORGIVE....................31

CHAPTER SIX HE'S MY BROTHER 37

CHAPTER SEVEN LORD, LET MY LIFE STAND FOR
SOMETHING..43

CHAPTER EIGHT DARKNESS BEFORE THE DAWN 67

CHAPTER NINE "THERE CANNOT BE A RESURRECTION,
IF THERE HAS NOT BEEN A DEATH." 85

FORWARD

"Whoso findeth a wife, findeth a good thing and obtaineth favor of the Lord." (Proverbs 18:22)

The things that you are about to hear are true. I record this with much sorrow and regret for the things that took place in my life and my marriage. I can only tell you that my life was out of control. I did not know the Lord and I was foolish in a lot of areas of my life. I made errors in judgment, some bad choices and had an unrealistic view of life. I was blinded by Satan's lies – that you only live once – and by my own pride, as far as my manhood was concerned. I wanted my cake and ice cream too. I hurt a lot of people, especially my wife who stood beside me putting up with my mess when she could have walked away from me so many times. I was ruthless at times, and I caused her so much pain. I put her through a whole lot but she was always in my corner praying for me. I used to get so angry with her for praying for me. That is just how sick I was, not realizing that it was her prayers that covered me. It hurts me and it embarrasses me to see what I used to be. There are a lot of horrible stories that my wife could have written about in this book, but because of who she is, a loving, tenderhearted and compassionate person, she chose not to because of her love, respect and honor for me. I want to say that I do not have any excuse for the things that I have said or done. All I can say is that I am not that same man today. I have a clearer vision of who I am. And I have accepted

Jesus Christ as my Lord and Savior. I love him and praise him that I am not the man that I used to be. I praise God for saving me and I thank the Lord for my wife because if anyone ever had the right to hate anyone, it would be her but she did not. She chose to love rather than hate. She chose good over evil. She only embraced the challenge and believed God to save me and change my heart. She is truly a woman of God, and she loves the Lord. I have come to realize that all I have in this life is the Lord and my wife. When my family and friends were not there for me, I could always call my wife or go to her and she would be there for me. No matter how bad I had hurt her, she would still help me. I just want to tell her how much I love her, how much I appreciate her, how I thank her for praying for me, forgiving me for hurting her and for giving our marriage another chance. You see I have said a lot of things about my wife to my children, family and friends that are not true. I caused them to dislike her and turn away from her to the point that they were angry with me for going back to her but they did not know the things that I said to them was only a cover-up for what I was doing so they would not know the truth about how sick I really was and how desperately I needed help to be set free. I want my children and family to know that I was wrong for what I have done and I am sorry for the pain that I have caused them. I am sorry that I destroyed relationships between them and my wife but most of all, I am grateful that my wife understood why I did the things that I did and that she has forgiven all. The Lord has healed our relationship and he has restored our marriage. He has given us a deeper love for each other and a greater respect for one another. We have agreed to tell our story so that it may help other couples to stand and believe the Lord for their marriage when things seem impossible. God will do just what he said he would do. I know that there will be some who still won't believe the things that I am saying and some who will harbor resentment in their heart towards us but if the truth be told, that's their problem. I have taken mine before the Lord and if they need to hold on to unforgiveness, that's between them and the Lord.

My wife's book tells the story of how we overcame the attack on our marriage and how the Lord brought us back together, restored our marriage and now how he is moving in every area of our lives. Glory to God. Lastly I want to say to the men that might be battling with the works of the flesh as I was: if you have a good wife, learn from my mistakes. If God has given you a godly wife, love and honor her, as Christ loved the Church. Get saved and live your life for the Lord. Your life will never be the same again because, "They that walk in the Spirit, shall not fulfill the lust of the Flesh." (Galatians 5:16) Amen!

Bobby West, Sr.

INTRODUCTION

Broken Pieces, Shattered Dreams and Swerved Relationships

A famous writer penned a great rhyme about an egg that was broken. He wrote these words:

> Humpty Dumpty sat on the wall,
> Humpty Dumpty had a great fall,
> All the king's horses, and all the king's men
> Couldn't put Humpty together again.

And so it is in our lives, all the powerful people in the world will not be able to put us back together again; only God can, God honors brokenness and he will mend our broken hearts and bind up all our wounds.

The word of David is recorded in the Psalms after he repented before the Lord. "Create in me a clean heart, O' God, and renew a right spirit within me." David knew what would please the Lord. He said. "For thou desirest not sacrifice; else would I give it; thou delightest not burnt offering. The sacrifices of God are a broken spirit, and a broken and contrite heart, O' God, thou wilt not despise." (Psalm 51:10, 16, 17)

God honors humility and brokenness. We have to remember when we are in the wilderness not to think about the wilderness; rather we should think about and focus on where the Lord is taking us. Think about the Promised Land he is taking you to, not the wilderness you are going through. The Promised Land should be your focus, not the wilderness. The Apostle Paul said, "If there is anything good, think on that."

So many times we think we are "catching hell" going through our trials. But the next time you are tempted to feel that way, remember Jesus has the keys to hell! Amen.

CHAPTER ONE
BROKENESS

"Every branch that bears fruit he purgeth it, that it may bring forth more fruit." (John 15:2)

Broken pieces are fragments that God can use. There were fragments that were taken up after Jesus had fed a great multitude of four thousand men (plus women and children) using a few loaves of bread and a few little fishes. After he had given thanks and broken them, he gave to his disciples and the disciples gave to the multitude. After they had eaten and were full, they took up seven baskets full of broken meat. When he broke five loaves of bread to feed the thousands, there were twelve baskets full of fragments taken up after all had eaten and were full. God has an amazing anointing for what can be done with the fragments that are left over. And so it is with the broken pieces in our lives. When we are going through the many trials that life brings our way, we have to always remember, "All things are possible to him that believeth." (Mark 9:23) He can take <u>nothing</u> and make <u>something</u> out of it, if you will believe.

As I sat looking out of my window, the rain fell down to the earth. Raindrops streamed down the windowpane, as tears ran down my face. I cried out, "Lord, let my life stand for something." Filled with sorrow and brokenness I said, "Lord, here I am fifty years old, half of a hundred; what have I accomplished? What have I done with

1

my life?" Silence flooded the room. I listened attentively to hear the Lord speak, but to no avail. The silence remained. As I stared out of my window on this dreary day, I saw the squirrels playing on the ground. I saw all types of birds – robins, blackburnian warbles, ruby crowned kinglet, mockingbird, cardinal, brown thrasher, free sparrow, redstart, roller and a blue jay. There were all types of birds jumping around on the ground, that I'd never seen there before in my front yard. I sat there amazed at their beauty and their carefree lives. I was feeling financial hardships, a lack of resources to meet financial obligations in paying my bills and meeting my own personal needs. There were so many things that I wanted to do for the Kingdom of God, but because there was a lack of resources I couldn't get the job done. I was faithful in tithing, giving and sowing seeds. I was living a holy life before the Lord. I was walking upright in his word and keeping his commandments. Yet, I was struggling in every area of my life except my walk with the lord. I was crying out to him and my heart was so heavy because I wanted to do so much more for him, and I was tired of living the way I was, struggling for the mere necessities. For as much as I desired to pay my bills and <u>do</u> for the Lord, there was not a manifestation. As I stood silently before the Lord, scriptures began to flood my spirit. "Behold the fowls of the air, for they sow not, neither do they reap, yet your heavenly Father feedeth them. Are ye not much better than they? Therefore, take no thought for the morrow: For the morrow shall take thought for the things of itself. Sufficient unto the day is the evil thereof." (Matt 6:26, 34) "Be silent to the Lord, and wait patiently for him." (Psalm 37:7) "In quietness and confidence shall be your strength." (Isaiah 30:15) "Seek ye first the kingdom of God, and his righteousness, and all these things shall be added unto you." (Matt 6:33). "I can do all things through Christ which strengthened me. But my God shall supply all my needs according to his riches in glory by Christ Jesus." (Philippians 4:13, 19) "No weapon that is formed against me shall prosper, and every tongue that shall rise against me in judgment shall be condemned. This is the heritage of the servants of the Lord, and their righteousness is of me, and the work that I do shall he do also; and greater works than these shall he do because I go unto my father." (John 14:12) "I am more than a conqueror through him that love me." (Rom 8:37) "Being confident of this very thing, which he has begun a great work in you will perform it until the day of Jesus Christ." (Philippians 1:6) "Count it all joy." (James 1:2) "The joy of the lord is your strength." (Ned. 8:10) "It is God which worketh in you both to will and to do of his good pleasure." (Philippians 2:13) "Those things that were gain to me, those I count loss for Christ, not because I desire a gift, but I desire fruit that may abound to your account." (Philippians 3:7 and Philippians 4:17) The word just arose in my spirit. It was as sheets of pages being thrown out of a book, blowing in the wind of my mind, page after page. Then I noticed the wind picking up and in the distance I noticed how it began to blow the trees. When I got a closer look I noticed that only a few trees was moving, and I said: *Lord, why is that so?* And He said, "It's not the wind; the wind is blowing on them all." He said, "Some of them are more sensitive to the moving of my spirit than others. Some of them willfully and freely praise me while others are strong and stout hearted and refuse to move and praise me. They are like my people. They have grown hard and cold toward me. Their hearts are waxed cold in my presence." It was then that I understood why it was that when we are in a powerful anointing service not everyone is touched. It is because their heart is waxed cold toward God, and they look in astonishment when people are hit and fall by the power of God. They completely do not understand it and have no idea what is taking place in the spirit realm. You see, it was the same wind that blew on all the trees but not all of them moved with the wind. It is the same anointing that removes the burden and destroys the yoke in our lives yet everyone is not set free. Why? I believe it has a lot to do with believing, receiving and praise.

When Paul and Silas were cast into prison after praying for a young damsel possessed with a demonic spirit, they were beaten unmercifully, then thrown into prison. They began to pray and sing praises unto God. They were bound with shackles on their feet and fast in the stocks. They were not only in prison but also in bondage at the mercy of the prison guards. However, Paul and Silas did not see it that way. They began to sing, praising God. They did not sing because they were happy, but they sang because they were free. No jail cell or chains could ever hold their spirits. They chose to pray and praise God rather than to have a pity party in prison. When the Lord revealed that to me, I realized that I did not have to allow my financial dilemma to dictate who I am in Christ Jesus. No, my righteousness in itself is nothing, but in Christ Jesus, my righteousness is everything!

So that day from my window, the Lord spoke loud and clear not to look at my situation but to look at my designation. He reminded me through nature that it did not matter how small we are or what our cares are, he is a God that will supply our every need day by day. Animals do not worry about what they will eat or where they will sleep; but their needs are always met in Christ Jesus.

Jesus demonstrated his love and compassion over and over as he walked the face of the earth healing and delivering multitudes. He healed broken hearts, broken spirits and shattered dreams. He will not only change you but he will rearrange you to get you to the point where you need to be in him. Through the wilderness, you will understand along the lonely path; you will better understand that the easiest path is not always the best path. Waiting and abiding in the presence of the Lord, only you can go through this process. Humility and total submission and a heart after God are the only things that will get you through the process. A famous songwriter wrote, "I sing because I am happy, I sing because I am free. His eyes is on the sparrow, and I know that he watches me."

I have learned when you seem to be at your very worst, things will suddenly take a nosedive. When you have reached "rock bottom," when you are at "ground zero," with all of your brokenness, with all your hurts and pains, when all of your dreams are shattered, when all of the vows and promises have been broken, when all of the people you looked up to and loved let you down, turned their backs on you and walked away, when people you thought were your friends turn against you; when you thought they were for you, when lies, deceptions and persecution finally take a toll on you and your heart and soul are wounded, when your spirit is crushed and you have been counted out of the race as the hare counted the tortoise out, that's when God will step in and do the impossible. "There is a Balm in Gilead and a Healing for your Soul."

There is a beautiful story about "The Hare and the Tortoise." The hare always boasted about his speed to other animals. He loved to brag about how fast he could run and no one could beat him in a race. One day, he challenged a tortoise to race against him for the fun of it. The tortoise accepted his challenge. To the hare, it was a good joke. He said he could dance a ring around the tortoise all the way and still win the race. The race was on. The hare quickly dashed off out of sight but soon decided to stop and rest. He even took a nap to show his contempt for the tortoise. But the tortoise just kept right on moving; he plodded on and on, passing the hare who was napping in the bush along the way. When the hare finally awoke, he saw the tortoise nearing the finish line. He ran as fast as his little legs would take him, but it was not working. He could not make up the time and distance he had lost. Tired as he was, the tortoise kept his pace, plodding to the finish line to win the race.

I know in my spirit that the hare must have felt like a fool, seeing the tortoise crossing the finish line. I can imagine in my mind that the Tortoise must have been quoting this scripture to himself, encouraging himself to press on toward the mark. "The race is not to the swift nor the battle to the strong, neither yet bread to the wise, nor yet riches to men of understanding, nor yet favor to men of skill; but time and chance happened to them all." (Ecclesiastes 9:11) We have to be persistent about the Kingdom of God. We have to stay the course. Though the path may not be easy, continue to press toward the mark.

We must have faith in God. The Bible tells us that, "Without faith, it is impossible to please him: for he that cometh to God must believe that he is a rewarder of them that diligently seek him." (Hebrews 11:6) We cannot afford to lie down and take a spiritual nap. Our adversary is watching, and he is not going to fall asleep. He is waiting for us to fall away so that he may tear us into tiny pieces – so he can devour us. It is a price we cannot afford to pay.

The Bible tells us that when we have done all we can do to stand, then stand some more. When Moses was leading the Israelites out of Egypt, it was a great task. Though the Israelites wanted to be free, they did not want to do what was right. They would not listen to Moses and they were not ready to follow leadership, nor submit to authority. They were a disobedient, greedy and rebellious people. They hungered after pleasure and desired to please their flesh. They were full of lasciviousness and all the work of the flesh. They mumbled and grumbled, complaining constantly about any and every thing.

The weight was heavy upon Moses' shoulders and he went to the Lord for help. He said, "Lord, why did you pick me, to burden me with a people like this?" Moses began to cry out to the Lord for help. He said, "I can't carry this matter by myself; and if you are not going to help me, kill me right now; it will be a kindness. Let me out of this impossible situation." It's clear that Moses was catching it from the people, to say the least. So the Lord told Moses to call a meeting and select for himself seventy elders of Israel to help him to carry the burden of the people. Yet, while Moses was having the meeting with the seventy elders in the tabernacle, (as the spirit came down and rested upon them,) there were two men outside in the camp. I believe that these men had been hungry for the spirit of the Lord to touch them and they desired to be used by the Lord. They were not chosen by Moses to be the elders in the meeting. Yet God knew their hearts and he touched them and filled them with his spirit also. They begin to prophesy in the camp, as did the seventy elders when the spirit rested upon them.

There arose jealousy in the camp when some young men heard that the two men prophesied there. They ran and told Moses what was taking place. Moses never lost his cool. Moses knew who he was in Christ Jesus. He did not fear God, blessing other people with his gifts. Moses realized that those gifts came from the Lord, not him, and he had nothing to fear. He was not jealous of these two men.

Joshua, a close servant of Moses, wanted to protect Moses and make them stop. Joshua was also jealous of these men's gifts and he wanted these gifts to belong to the one he thought was worthy of these gifts. He wanted Moses to forbid them to speak or be used by

God. Moses, still cool and calm, just said, "Are you jealous for my sake? I only wish that all of the Lord's people were prophets and the Lord would put his spirit upon them. Then Moses turned and walked away returning back to the camp."

The point to this story is this: Moses knew his righteousness in Christ Jesus and he was sure who he was. He did not need to be upset or envious of the gifts of God or his people. He was glad to see these men touched, and he desired to see more of the people hungry and thirsty after God's righteousness. He indeed wanted them to catch the vision so that the burden would not be so heavy upon his shoulders. (Numbers 11:10-29)

When we are going through suffering and persecution for Christ's sake, we don't have to be poor, little, pitiful Christians. We have power and authority within us. The Bible calls us *Blessed* if we are insulted because of his name and that when we suffer for him in our flesh, we are just beginning to live with him eternally.

There is enough work for all of us to do for the Kingdom of God. There is enough Jesus for all of us. We do not have to be jealous of one another or the gifts of God. The Bible declares, "The Harvest is truly plenteous but the Laborers are few." Just as Moses learned to love despite all, he foresaw the coming of the cross and Jesus. He demonstrated love to the Israelites time after time. Jesus left us an example: when Jesus was in the Garden of Gethsemane praying, getting ready to be offered up for the whole world's sins. Peter, one of his disciples drew his sword and smote one of the High Priest's officer's ear off – cutting it and causing it to fall onto the ground. Jesus, filled with love and compassion, reached down and picked up the officer's ear and placed it back onto his head.

Jesus knew his purpose here on earth and he knew his time was up. He could not allow Peter, whom he loved so dearly, to hinder or stop the scriptures from being fulfilled. He was too close to allow unforgiveness, hatred and bitterness to stop him from doing his Father's will.

He told Peter to "put up his sword into the sheath; the cup which my Father hath given me, shall I not drink it?" (John 18:11) And even though Jesus knew he was on his way to the cross, he chose to forgive. He chose to love and not hate. Jesus knew when Judas returned with the High Priest soldiers that they would deliver him up to the High Priest. But <u>Jesus still healed</u> the soldier's ear. He could not leave it on his record that he refused to heal. <u>He still had to HEAL.</u> It was in his nature. It did not matter what had taken place; Jesus still had to heal him.

When Jesus was on the cross, Jesus still pled for the thieves' souls, even while he hung there on the cross. He said, "Father, forgive them for they know not what they do." Even then, being mocked and crucified, Jesus heard and answered prayers. Hanging there between two thieves, he was mocked by one while the other repented of his sins. <u>Jesus Still Had To Save Him; He Could Not Refuse Him His Salvation</u>. The thief said, "Jesus, Lord, remember me when thou comest into thy kingdom," and Jesus said unto him, "Verily I say unto thee, today, shalt thou be with me in paradise." (Luke 23: 42-43)

Jesus <u>still forgave and saved souls</u>. The scripture records that it was about the sixth hour, just three hours before Jesus gave up the ghost, that he was <u>still forgiving and saving souls</u>. What an awesome and powerful testimony Jesus left behind for us to follow.

In this beautiful story, we learn the power of love, the reward of forgiveness and the compassion we possess inside of us when we chose love and not hate. We see the strength in weakness when we allow the Lord to break us and humble us. We see from the cross as Jesus' body and spirit was being broken, he was – at the same time – being made every way whole. God will honor your brokenness with far more than rubies or pearls, with more than all that this life has to offer you or give to you. He tells us to, "Come unto me all ye that labor and are heavy laden and learn of me; for I am meek and lowly in heart and ye shall find rest for your souls, for my yoke is easy and my burden is light." (Matthew 11:28-30)

CHAPTER TWO
FRIENDLY FIRE

"Trust ye not in a friend, put ye not confidence in a guide. Keep the doors of thy mouth from her that lieth in thy bosom. For the son dishonoureth the Father, the daughter riseth up against her mother, the daughter-in-law against her mother-in-law, a man's enemies are the men of his own house." (Micah 7:5-6)

Sometimes the fiery darts of the enemy are "friendly fire" from your loved ones and the people closest to you. It is not always the enemy that want to see harm befall you. Saul was jealous of David for killing ten thousand Philistines (while Saul only killed thousands.) Saul was very angry because the people praised David for such an outstanding job, and the women went wild over David. The Bible says that, "They even came out of the cities of Israel singing and dancing to meet David with taborets, with joy and with instruments of music and they asked one another saying, Saul has slain his thousands and David his ten thousands. Saul was very wroth and displeased. *They have ascribed unto David ten thousand and they have ascribed but a thousand; what can he have more but the kingdom?* And Saul eyed David from that day forward." From that time on, Saul desired David's life. He was afraid that David would take his place and his position because he knew that the Lord was with David. Saul also knew that the Lord had departed from him. Not once but twice did Saul try to set David up to be killed, but the Lord was still with David. However, the scripture says, "David behaved himself wisely – David behaved himself wisely in all his ways – and David behaved himself more wisely than all the servants of Saul." (1ˢᵗ Samuel 18:5, 14, 30)

Sometimes when you are being fired upon it's best not to fire back. Simply leave it alone or just walk away. Wisdom must be applied in every area of our lives. Let's take a close look at David, and how he used wisdom in his life:

1. By fleeing (1ˢᵗ Samuel 19:18-23);
2. By not talking. Sometimes it is wise to say only a few words or no words at all. (1ˢᵗ Samuel 26:4-25);
3. By not touching them. (1ˢᵗ Samuel 24:1-10);
4. By praying for them. David continuously blessed the Lord with thanksgiving in his heart at all times for Saul and his enemies.

A lot of times we cannot choose the situations that we are in, nor can we control them. But we can choose how we are going to respond to them. You have to willfully choose to control your emotions. One of Satan's most powerful tools is to distract you from the will of God. He knows that if he can cause you to become offended, it will take your focus off of God. We must keep our eyes on the Lord no matter the cost. We must not act as the world would act or react as they would react; rather learn to be vigilant, watching and praying, pulling down strongholds and casting down every imagination that exalts itself against the Word of God. We must discipline our flesh in the areas of hurt and frustration, knowing the true meaning of meekness and longsuffering. To humble ourselves under the mighty hand of God assures us of who we are in Christ Jesus: more than conquerors. The Apostle Peter wrote, "But the God of all grace, who hath called us unto his eternal glory by Christ Jesus, after that ye have suffered a while, make you perfect, establish, strengthen and settle you." (1ˢᵗ Peter 5:10)

Therefore, knowing our character is not determined by what we say or do when we are hurt or wronged by someone else – but rather by what we do not do when we are wrongfully attacked and wounded unjustly – we have to learn to overcome our hurts, our disappointments and pride. We have to choose to willingly forgive. We have to overcome evil with good. Know who you are fighting, "For we wrestle not against flesh and blood, but against principalities, against powers, against the rulers of the darkness of this world, against spiritual wickedness in high places." (Ephesians 6:12)

There are also times in our walk with the Lord when the Lord begins to cut things, places and people off from us. Respectfully, we have to be able to discern what the Lord is doing. We see how the Lord took David through the process of swerving relationships with Saul and Jonathan. No matter how David wanted to honor Saul by continuing to serve him, he discerned the time was upon him to depart from Saul's presence. The scripture tells us while David was very loyal to Saul in serving him, an evil spirit came from God upon Saul while David played music with his hands to calm Saul's spirit. Saul desired to kill David with a javelin because he envied the Lord's presence with David. Saul was so displeased with him until he made David his captain over a thousand soldiers just to get rid of him. David discerned the jealousy of Saul toward him. David avoided Saul's presence, not once but twice. Yet, the scriptures say David behaved himself wisely in all his ways; and the Lord was with him. Wherefore, when Saul saw that David behaved himself very wisely, he was afraid of David. (1st Samuel 18:8-15)

Nevertheless, Saul's heart was still fixed on killing David. He even wanted his son Jonathan to be a part of murdering him. It's funny – when one person does not like you or hates you – they want to draw their whole family into it so they may hate you also. They will influence other people to hate you, just because they have aught against you. Well, Jonathan did not want David's innocent blood on his hands. Jonathan had a covenant with David and he could not deny him. Jonathan spoke good of David to his father and said, "Let not the king sin against his servant David, because his works have been very good for he did put his life in his hand and slew the Philistine for you. But the evil spirit from the Lord was upon Saul as he sat in his house with his javelin in his hand. Saul sought to smite

David to the wall with the javelin but David slipped away out of Saul's presence, fled and escaped that night."

Sometimes you have to run for your life when you are serving God, not because of your badness but because of your goodness. We see in the scripture what envy and jealousy can do to even a man of God. Saul saw things in David that really were not there. Because he was blinded with jealousy and fear of the people's love for David and the Lord's hands being upon David's life, he convinced himself that David was his enemy when in fact David was on his side. This was friendly fire. The Bible tells us that Saul was so disturbed that he went searching for David; he inquired where Samuel and David were. Someone replied, "They are at Naioth and Ramah, he stripped off his clothes and prophesied before Samuel. Then laid down naked all that day and all that night. Wherefore, they said, Is Saul also among the prophets? (1st Samuel 19)

We see friendly fire upon David from relationships. Micah 7:6, "A man's enemies are the men of his own house." Yet, it is recorded in 1st Samuel 18:30, "David behaved himself more wisely than ALL the servants of Saul; so that his name was much set by." Through all the things David had to endure, he never lost his faith in God. He still preferred to flee Saul's presence rather than to touch the anointing on Saul's life. We also saw that the Lord caused the evil spirit to come upon Saul, not as one might conclude to be Satan. It is my belief that the Lord had a plan for David's life that many around him could see. Yet, not everyone around him could see it, especially the one's closest to him in his family. They looked upon him as the least out of his seven brothers, a keeper of sheep from the backside of the woods. No one expected him to ever amount to anything. A poor, little shepherd boy. But God had other plans for David's life; still David had to go through the process of being stripped and broken of people, places and things so that the Lord could move him to the next level of his calling. The Lord had to swerve David's relationship with Saul in order for David to go to the next level. We must realize that sometimes when we think Satan is doing things in our lives to cause a person to act as they do, it might be God that is driving you out into new territory for the work of the Kingdom.

We have to realize that it is not about us; it is all about Kingdom building. Paul wrote in Roman 11:28-29, "As concerning the gospel, they are enemies for your sakes; but as touching the election they are beloved for the Father's sakes, for the gifts and calling of God are without repentance."

Now in the process of God getting David to where he wanted him, David had to also swerve the relationship he had with his best friend Jonathan. Serving God is not without sacrifices. David records in Psalm 4:3-5, "But know that the Lord hath set apart him that is godly for himself. The Lord will hear when I call unto him. Stand in awe and sin not. Commune with your own heart upon your bed and be still. Se-lah. Offer the sacrifices of righteousness and put your trust in the Lord." The scripture tells us that Jonathan, the son of Saul, was so knitted with the soul of David, that he loved David as he loved his own soul. Jonathan made a covenant with David because he loved him as his own soul. Jonathan stripped himself of the robe that was upon him and gave it to David – even his sword, his bow and his girdle. (1st Samuel 18:1-4)

There will be times when the Lord will require relationship "swerves" that will be painful to bear, as he calls you to come from out among them and sends you in another direction to do his will. As the Lord moved David out into new territory in the Cave Adullam, the Lord made him to be a captain over four hundred men who were distressed, in debt and discontented, who had gathered themselves together in a cave. God was moving David because his job was finished with Saul and the Philistine. These men needed him to lead and guide them. That is how the Lord usually works. He always has a ram in the bush, caught for us and to take our place so that we will not be slaughtered.

Though this company of people was much smaller than the army of men of war he had lead in the past, David was not moved by the size of men but rather by the needs in their lives, which were many. The prophet Zechariah wrote, "Who hath despised the day of small things?" (Zechariah 4:10) The Lord is not impressed with where we were born nor where we came from, nor who our ancestors are, how much money we have or our social status. He is not moved by any of that. If God can use a jackass to warn a prophet (causing the ass to speak, telling him what lay before him, Numbers 22:20 - 25) and a chicken to tell Peter (I told you so that before the cock crowed, that you would deny the Lord thrice, Matthew 26:75), surely he can use you and me. Who are we to pick and choose who God can and cannot use for his glory? "For there is no respecter of persons with God."

John declared, "For now that the spirit of truth has come into the world whom the world cannot receive because it seeth him not, neither knoweth him; but ye know him for he dwelleth with you and shall be in you. Howbeit when he, the spirit of truth is come, he will guide you into all truth; for he shall not speak of himself, but whatsoever he shall hear, that shall he speak and he will shew you things to come. For there is no respect of persons with God." And the truth of the matter is, it is going to cost you everything to walk close with the Lord. God has commanded us to love. God has commanded us to keep his commandments; he said those that keep his commandments love him and his Father. He said if we love him, we will keep his commandments. In doing this, you will have fulfilled the royal law according to the Scripture. Thou shalt love thy neighbor as thyself; ye do well.

John 16:1-4 says, "These things have I spoken unto you, that you should not be offended. They shall put you out of the synagogues; yea the time cometh that whosoever killed you will think that he doeth God's service. And those things will they do unto you, because they have not known the Father, nor me. But these things I said not unto you at the beginning, because I was with you." Esaias had prophesied these things and Jesus said that the prophecy would be fulfilled. Jesus withdrew himself from them for a while, hiding from them. Many could not believe because their eyes had been blinded, their heart had been hardened, that they could not see with their eyes nor understand with their hearts. They believed the chief rulers and, because of the Pharisees, they did not confess Jesus. They could not be converted, nor healed, for they were afraid that they would be put out of the synagogue for they loved the praises of men more than the praise of God. (John 12:38-43)

While David humbly submitted to Saul, he knew he had to obey the one who had the rule over him; he submitted himself to Saul. God raised David up for honoring his word. God's word commands us to obey those who have the rule over us and submit ourselves for they watch for our souls as they that must give account that they may do it with joy and not with grief, for that is unprofitable for us. (Hebrew 13:17) Yield peaceable fruit of righteousness; follow peace with all men and holiness. David wrote, "How good and how pleasant it is for brethren to dwell together in unity." (Psalm 133:11)

Sometimes we start out with good intentions and "SELF" gets into the way. We begin to exalt ourselves and not God. Then, God cannot use us because he cannot trust us with his anointing. The key is staying humble before the Lord. Samuel was so hurt over the mess that Saul had made when he sent him to smite the Amalek and destroy all that they had. Samuel instructed Saul to spare not a one, to slay the men and women, the children and the infants, to kill their ox, the sheep, the camel and the ass. But Saul did only part of what he was told to do. Ultimately it cost him his friendship with Samuel and his fellowship with the Lord. Saul's act of disobedience was the cause of Samuel's being broken into pieces, his dreams shattered and their relationship being swerved. "Then came the word of the Lord unto Samuel saying, it repenteth me that I have set up Saul to be king; for he is turned back from following me and hath not performed my commandments and it grieved Samuel. He cried unto the Lord all night and Samuel came no more to see Saul until the day of his death. Nevertheless, Samuel mourned for Saul and the Lord repented that he had made Saul king over Israel."

When there is jealousy in the camp, whether it is on your job, in your home, in the church or in our family, we cannot act like the world acts. God has called us to a higher standard. When the Lord told Moses to choose seventy elders of Israel because the load was too heavy for him to carry alone, there arose jealousy in the camp. The scripture tells us in the book of Numbers 11:10-29, "There were two men in the camp, one by the name of Eldad and the other was named Medad. The spirit of the Lord rested upon them and they were not chosen by Moses to be elders, yet God's spirit rested upon them outside of the camp and they began to prophesy in the camp. Another young man in the camp heard of it and ran to report it to Moses telling him that they prophesy in the camp. He wanted Moses to forbid them to prophesy. However, Moses knew the young man's heart and said to him, Enviest thou for my sake? Would God that all the Lord's people were prophets and that the Lord would put his spirit upon them?" Moses simply got up and walked away and went back into the camp. Moses knew it was just jealousy. We cannot afford the spirit of jealousy, bitterness, strife and unforgiveness. It's too high a price to pay.

Moses realized that the devil sends people close to him to cause confusion. This young man was very close to Moses, and he was a servant of Moses along with Joshua. Nevertheless, he allowed the devil to use him with envy. This is one of the things that the people of God had to closely guard their hearts against. I like the way Proverbs 4:23 records it in the Amplified Bible, "Keep and guard your heart with vigilance and above all that you guard, for out of it flows the springs of life." The devil does not care whom he uses. He does not care if you love the Lord. All that he wants is a little crack to come in, in order to get a stronghold. We must not give any room for the devil to come in. No, not one inch.

CHAPTER THREE
HOW DO YOU PATCH THE TITANIC?

"With loving-kindness have I drawn thee." (Jeremiah 31:3) God has called us with a holy call, a call of righteousness. He tells us in his word that, "The eyes of the Lord run to and fro throughout the whole earth, to shew himself strong on behalf of them whose heart is perfect toward him." (2nd Chronicles 16:9)

We are living in a time where men and women will sell their bodies for the love of money. Some will prostitute their bodies, some will prostitute their souls and some will prostitute the word and the gifts of God.

We are living in a time when men of the cross have fallen prey to the lust of the flesh. Paul wrote to the Church of Rome that, "The gifts and calling of God are without repentance." (Romans 11:29) When you turn on the television, we see all over the news time and time again, men of the cross being accused of sexual immorality, fraud, child abuse and sexual molestation under the cover of "In the name of Jesus." False prophets are rising up everywhere, deceiving many and taking the body of Christ unaware. Paul goes on to tell us in Roman 12: 1-3, "I beseech you therefore brethren, by the mercies of God, that ye present your bodies a living sacrifice, holy, acceptable unto God, which is your reasonable service. And be not conformed to this world: but be ye transformed by the renewing of your mind, that ye may prove what is that good, and acceptable, and perfect will of God. For I say through the grace given unto me, to every man that is among you, not to think of himself more highly than he ought to think; but to think soberly, according as God hath dealt to every man the measure of faith."

So many have been led away by false prophets and unholy men who confess to be called of God. Some are teaching that homosexuality is all right by saying, "God created them that way." But God would not have us to be ignorant of the devices of the devil. God is not double minded and he surely is not schizophrenic. He tells us in the book of James 1: 5, 6 & 8, "If any man lack wisdom, let him ask of God, that giveth to all men liberally and upbraideth not; and it shall be given him. A double minded man is unstable in all of his ways. For he that wavereth is like a wave of the sea driven with the wind and tossed." For he cannot receive the goodness of God. No, not anything. God's word is true and God's word is pure. He said, "If any man desire the office of a Bishop, he desires a good work." So, we clearly see that it is not the word of the Lord that is corrupt. It is people who corrupt God's word.

Timothy wrote, "In latter times some shall depart from the faith, giving heed to seducing spirits and doctrines of devils, speaking lies in hypocrisy and having their consciences seared with a hot iron." God is not confused. He was not confused when he gave Moses his law. His law was clear and firm. He did not waver in his instructions to Moses to keep the commandments, the statutes and the judgments that we shall live by, that we may observe and do them. Paul wrote to Timothy, "That the law is good, if a man use it lawfully." We have to be careful not to be deceived by philosophy, traditions of men and false doctrine, but to stay steadfast in the faith.

Homosexuality has become a thing of the "now" where men and women have not discerned the time in which we are living in. They use vain excuses like *God made me this way* or *I have always been a female but I was born a male*. This is an unclean spirit through the lust of the flesh where men and women dishonor their own bodies with corruptible and unnatural desires. "Who changed the truth of God into a lie." Was God a madman when he created man and mistakenly crisscrossed the male and female genitals spiritually, emotionally and physically? Did he hide something deep, deep down on the inside of them that would birth within after they are born to tell them God had made a mistake and had put them in the wrong body and it is screaming and crying to get out. *Let me out!!! Let me out!!!*

No, I think not. God knew good and well what he was doing. The prophet Jeremiah wrote, "Then the word of the Lord came unto me saying, before I formed thee in the belly I knew thee; and before thou camest forth out of the womb I sanctified thee and I ordained thee a prophet unto the nations." In the very beginning in the book of Genesis 1:27, the word says, "So God created man in his own image in the image of God created he him; male and female created he them." So we see God was not confused. God did not crisscross any of us. Not only did he not crisscross man, he did not even crisscross the animals, the plants, trees nor anything that creepeth upon the earth. It is even more clear throughout the whole chapter of Genesis 1. Whatever God said, that is what it was. God spoke and it was. It was manifested into existence, just as he said. So, when he said man, he did not crisscross the body of a man with the emotions of a women, nor did he say *Let us create man in our image* and then put a woman in the inside of him or vice versa. No, what he did say was, "Let us make man in our image, after our likeness–so God created man in his image, in the image of God created he him; male and female created he them." (Genesis 1:26, 27) God was not confused; God was clear; He was precise and to the point when he spoke a thing to be a thing, that was what he meant for it to be. When He said, "Let there be light," he did not say let there be light and the darkness remained. The scripture says, "And God said, let there be light and there was light." It was not half-light and half darkness. (Genesis 1:3) Genesis 1:4, 5 goes on to say, "And God saw the light, that it was good and God divided the light from darkness. And God called the light day and the darkness he called night." There is no excuse, nor is there any exception. He said everything he made was good. So if anything is contrary to what God said, it is evil: For God did not create the evil in it. The evil came from men's hearts and was birthed out of the lust of the flesh. God did not orchestrate it. "Let no man say when he is tempted, I am tempted with evil, neither tempteth he any man: But every man is tempted when he is drawn away of his own lust and enticed. Then when lust hath conceived, it bringeth forth sin: and sin, when it if finished, bringeth forth death. Do not err, my beloved brethren, every good gift and every perfect gift is from above and cometh down from the Father of lights with whom is no variableness, neither shadow of turning." (James 1: 13-17)

This is an unclean spirit through the lust of the flesh conceived in men hearts. "For out of the abundance of the heart, the mouth speaks." Men and women chose to dishonor God and their own bodies with corruptible and unnatural desires. Who changed the truth of God into a lie? God was not high on some kind of herb taken from the Garden of Eden. God knew the secrets of men hearts. Jeremiah said, "The heart is deceitful above all things and desperately wicked: Who can know it? God shall judge the secrets of men's hearts by Jesus Christ according to his gospel." Paul wrote, "For this cause God gave them up into vile affections: for even their women did change the natural use into that which is against nature. And likewise also the men leaving the natural use of the women, burned in their lust one toward another. Men with men working that which is unseemly, to receiving in themselves that recompense of their error which was meet. And they did not like to retain God in their knowledge. God gave them over to a reprobate mind, to do those things which are not convenient. Who knowing the judgment of God that they which commit such things are worthy of death, not only do the same, but have pleasure in them that do them." (Roman 1: 26, 27, 28, 32) Our bodies are the temples of the Holy Ghost. We are joined unto the Lord in one spirit. And we have been bought with a price, set apart for the Master's use – to glorify God. We are called to be servants of God, not men. This is a holy call. This is the price with which we have been bought.

The Lord is calling for a holy people to live clean and holy lives before the Lord and to come out from among them and be separated, vessels fit for the Master's use. The call of holiness is not doing what you want whenever you want. We do not belong to ourselves anymore. We cannot turn a deaf ear as the people of Egypt did when the Lord brought them out of bondage. They would not listen to Moses as the Lord spoke through him. "So I gave them up unto their own hearts lust and they walked in their own self counsels." (Psalm 81:12) And as a result of the hardness of their hearts, many perished while still wandering around in the wilderness, never getting to enter into the Promised Land. For in their own foolish hearts and vain imaginations, they professing themselves to be wise, become fools."

The things of God seemed to be foolishness to them and they could not discern them. God hid it from them because of their doubt and unbelief. Paul wrote in 1st Corinthians 1:25 - 29, "Because the foolishness of God is wiser than men; and the weakness of God is stronger than men. For ye see your calling, brethren how that not many wise men after the flesh. Not many mighty, not many noble are called. But God hath chosen the foolish things of the world to confound the wise and God hath chosen the weak things of the world to confound the things which are mighty and base things of the world and things which are despised hath God chosen. Yea, things which are not to bring to naught things that are: That no flesh should glory in his presence."

While some hide behind God, holding him hostage to fatten their bank accounts, others want the prestige of an elite social status but without the sweat of their brow. In the process, many will lose their souls not knowing they are on their way to hell. They are being deceived by false prophets, men who say they are called by God, who are supposed to be standing in the gap and watching over our souls. Yet, they cannot get a prayer off of the ground because of the lies they are living. They are robbing God and the people of God with divers lusts and corrupt minds. The house of worship has too often become a marketplace for buying and selling, not just material things but have quickly become a fashion place for marketing sex, high-class prostitution, adultery and business proposals.

When Jesus came into Jerusalem, he went into the temple and discovered moneychangers. He became so upset that he began to drive them out that bought and sold there. He said, "Is it not written, my house shall be called of all nations the house of prayer? But ye have made it a den of thieves." The Church, God's Holy temple, has been prostituted before the whole world. The Bible warns us in 2nd Timothy 3: 1-7, "This know also, that in the last days perilous times shall come, for men shall be lovers of their own selves, covetous, boasters, proud, blasphemers, disobedient to parents, unthankful, unholy, without natural affection, truce breakers, false accusers, incontinent, fierce, despisers of those that are good. Traitors, heady, high minded, lovers of pleasures more than lovers of God. Having a form of Godliness but denying the power thereof; from such turn away, for this sort are they which creep into houses and lead captive silly women laden with sins, led away with divers lusts, ever learning and never able to come to the knowledge of the truth." Peter wrote, "For the time is come that judgment must begin at the house of God and if it first begins at us what shall the end be of them that obey not the gospel of God? And if the righteousness scarcely be saved, where shall the ungodly and sinner appear?" (1st Peter 4:17-18) It's all got to stop, but when will it end? And how do you patch the Titanic? Jesus said he left us an example that we should follow in his steps; for us to be of one mind, having compassion one for another, love as brethren, be pitiful, be courteous, not rendering evil for evil or railing for railing: but contrariwise blessing, knowing that ye are there unto called, that ye should inherit a blessing. For he that will love life and see good days, let him refrain his tongue from evil and his lips that they speak no guile. Let him eschew evil and do well; let him seek peace and ensure it. For the eyes of the Lord are over the righteous and his ears are open unto their prayers but the face of the Lord is against them that do evil." (1st Peter 3:8-12)

How do you patch the Titanic? With love, repentance and with compassion. The Word of God is clear. "Whosoever hate his brother is a murderer— and he loves us with an everlasting love, with loving-kindness have I drawn thee."

How do you patch the Titanic? Paul wrote, "Owe no man anything but to love one another for he that loveth another hath fulfilled the Law." and, "By love serve one another."

How do you patch the Titanic? "Be not overcome by evil, but overcome evil with good."

How do you patch the Titanic? By "Forgetting those things which are behind and reaching forth unto those things which are before, to press toward the mark for the prize of the high calling of God in Christ Jesus."

How do you patch the Titanic? "If a man be overtaken in a fault which is spiritual, restore such a one in the spirit of meekness; considering thyself, lest thou also be tempted. Bear ye one another's burdens and so fulfill the law of Christ."

How do you patch the Titanic? "For God is not the author of confusion but of peace. Let us be not deceived; God is not mocked; for whatsoever a man soweth that shall he also reap—let us not be weary in well doing for in due season we shall reap, if we faint not. Let us do good unto all men, especially unto them who are of the household of faith."

There are so many ways that we can patch the Titanic such as with the fruit of the spirit, continuous prayers and supplication and the wisdom of God, by interceding for people, holding them up before the Lord and asking God to save them, bless them, etc.

Now here are a few ways that we cannot patch the Titanic, with envious, unforgiveness, bitterness, strife and by touching the anointing on a person's life. We must speak no evil, do no evil. Do not persecute others. Leave the judgment to God. "Vengeance belongeth unto me, I will recompense, saith the Lord and again the Lord shall judge his people."

CHAPTER FOUR
STAND FIRM IN YOUR FAITH

"And let them make me a sanctuary that I may dwell among them."

God is a rewarder to them that diligently seek him. He said after you have done the will of God, ye might receive the promise. Knowing the Lord, you shall receive the reward of the inheritance according to Colossians 3:24. The Lord knew that we had need of patience and confidence when the Apostle Paul wrote the Epistle to the Hebrews, "Cast not away therefore your confidence, which hath great recompense of reward. For ye have need of patience that after you have done the will of God, ye might receive the promise." (Hebrews 10:35-36)

God is calling for holiness. He is calling for us to be his people and he shall be our God. As we look around us today, we see every type of confusion and mess that is not of God. Men with men, women with women, children having babies and drugs everywhere. Innocent people being killed on the streets and in their homes from drive-by shootings. Gangs on the rise with more of the mafia style shootings than ever before. Guns falling into the hands of children and innocent children lives being snatched away in an instant because of guns in the homes. People fearing for their lives and their family's safety. Schools being attacked, no longer safe havens where children may learn anymore. Kids are being killed in the schools and on their campus in an alarming rate. Suicide and domestic violence in the homes, whole family lives taken in the blink of an eye. Snipers on the rampage; terrorists are everywhere. The economy is out of control. Gas and oil prices have skyrocketed. The stock market has taken a nosedive as the search for jobs increase with unemployment at an all time high. And last but not least, men desiring to play God, cloning human beings for self-gratification and glorifying themselves and not God. It is enough to make you sick. Every work of the flesh is manifested in the earth, and the saints of God have got to discern the time.

A world-renowned songwriter wrote a song about a Gambler. He said, "You got to know when to hold her, know when to fold her, know when to walk away, and know when to run." Though, he was talking about playing cards, gambling for money, we can apply it to our lives as well. When we are tempted or caught up in things that do not glorify God, we need to know when to hold our tongue, be quiet and shut up. We need to know when to fold our hands and walk away, and know when to come out from among them when God reveals a certain thing to you. We need to know when to run, to flee temptation when it comes. My mother use to always say, "A good run is better than a bad stand." In life I have found that to be true. We do not have to prove anything to anybody, but God. Someone might say, *Run? Oh no, not me!* But I say *Yes, run! Run for your life, so that your walk with the Lord maybe be pure and clean. Live a holy life before him and before man.*

In this song, the Gambler has sense enough to know when to wait, stop, walk away and even run. Christians have gotten to the point where they think like the world, they think they are Mt. Elbrus. "I am not going to take this or that" and "I am going to give them a piece of my mind" or "I am not going to move; let them move." But people, I tell you, when you know your flesh is weak in a certain area, why do you fool yourself that you can handle it? I cannot say that I have mastered every level. In some areas I am weak, and I am running for my life. I am not ashamed to say so. I think sometimes we get into more trouble when we become boastful and not humble, full of pride. And that allowed Satan to open a door and come in. And come in he will before a cat can wink his eye. I heard a preacher say, "Don't let Satan ride. If you let him ride, he'll want to drive." That's true; we must not give room to the devil. That's why the Bible tells us that we wrestle not against flesh and blood, but principalities. For the Lord has sent us forth as sheep in the midst of wolves, but we can be wise as a serpent, and harmless as a dove. (Matt10:16)

God is calling for true repentance. He is looking for women and men like his servant David, people after his own heart, not the hearts of men, not a heart full of idle words and empty promises. David said, "Create in me a clean heart, O God; and renew a right spirit within me." David feared the Lord, he wanted to be clean of all his sins, he said, "Purge me with hyssop, and I shall be clean, wash me and I shall be whiter than snow." David was willing to do whatever it took to get it right in the sight of God, because he had missed the mark and come short of God's will for his life. He quickly repented. He said "Cast me not away from thy presence; and take not thy holy spirit from me. Restore unto me the joy of thy salvation; and uphold me with thy free spirit." (Psalm 51:7, 10, 11, 12) Yet, today many think that they can live any kind of way and do anything and still be saved. It's sad that so many people are on their way to hell and they don't even know it. They truly believe that they are saved.

The Prophet Isaiah wrote, "Hell hath enlarged herself." Then he recorded, "Wherefore the Lord said, forasmuch as this people draw near me with their mouth and with their lips do honour me, but have removed their hearts far from me and their fear toward me is taught by the precepts of men." (Isaiah 5:14, 29:13) We have to cry out to the Lord, as Isaiah did when he was going through. "Be merciful unto me, O'God, be merciful unto me; for my soul trusteth in thee. My soul is among lions; and I lie even among them that are set on fire, even the sons of men whose teeth are spears and arrows and their tongue a sharp sword. But my heart is fixed. I will sing and praise thee." (Isaiah 57:1, 4, 7) Our hearts must be fixed on the Lord continually, daily.

One of the biggest downfalls of Christians in the Church is persecution by the Church. There is no love even in the Church.

The Church is supposed to be a healing place, both physically and spiritually. It should be a hospital for the wounded, but instead it has become a den of thieves, robbing God of his glory and prostituting his gifts for vainglory and money. I believe when Malachi wrote, "Will a man rob God?" It's much deeper than just tithes and offerings. We have robbed God of his glory, his character and his deity. Malachi declared, "And he shall turn the heart of the fathers to the children and the heart of the children to their fathers lest I come and smite the earth with a curse." (Malachi 4:8, 6) Why were these things so important for the Lord to say just before he closed the book of the Old Testament? I believe it was left there to have a profound effect in our hearing of his word. Malachi 3:15, 18 starts out by saying, "Behold, (listen) I will send my messenger, and he shall prepare the way before me." It is clear that Malachi's mission was repentance not just in tithes and offerings. Verse 5 makes it clearer, "And I will come near to you to judgment; and I will be a swift witness against the sorcerers, the adulterers, the false swearers, against those that oppress the hireling in his wages, the widow and the fatherless and them that turn aside the stranger from his right and fear not me, said the Lord of hosts. Then shall ye return and discern between the righteous and the wicked, between him that serveth God and him that serveth him not. Woe, to the house of God, judgment is at the door." It is repentance time and it must first begin at the house of faith. We must heal the wounded, the bruised and the broken hearted, the weak minded and the backsliders. Embrace the lost and reach out to the hurting and desolated. We must encourage the weak to stay strong and stay focused on God. Pray for those in captivity whether it is because of sins or whatever, we must reach the unreachable, tear down the boundaries and walls that separate us and keep us from serving the Lord. We must not fail because if we do then we have failed God – in his purpose for our lives. We cannot afford to fail God by picking and choosing when we want to serve God. We are living under an open heaven for souls to be harvested. We must labor even more now, taking the Gospel of Jesus Christ to a hurting world. We cannot leave anyone out. Matthew wrote in Matthew 25:45-46, "Inasmuch as ye did it not to one of the least of these, ye did it not to me and these shall go away into everlasting punishment but the righteous into life eternal."

We cannot be consumed with the cares of this world. God is bigger than that. We have to get our eyes off of "self" and back on God. When we are serving our flesh, we are walking in rebellion and we are out of the will of God. The Lord told Isaiah in a vision, "I have nourished and brought up children and they have rebelled against me. The ox knoweth his owner and the ass his master's crib, but Israel doth not know, my people doth not consider." He said, "Come now and let us reason together, saith the Lord: Though your sins be as scarlet, they shall be as white as snow; Though they be red like crimson, they shall be as wool and if you be willing and obedient, ye shall eat the good of the land; but if ye refuse and rebel, ye shall be devoured with the sword; for the mouth of the Lord hath spoken it." (Isaiah 1: 2, 3, 18, 19)

We have to spiritually discern the tactics of the enemy. We have to pray not to enter into temptation. The scripture teaches us to pray, "Lead us not into temptation, but deliver us from evil." We have steadied the course laid out for us by the Lord. For Proverbs tells us that, "There is a way that seem right to man, but the end therefore is death." (Proverbs 16:25) We have to be mindful that Jesus did not promise us that temptation would not come. He said, in his promises, in this world we would have trials and tribulation but be of good courage for he has already overcome the world and with that came a promise, "There hath no temptation taken you but such as in common to man, but God is faithful, who will not suffer you to be tempted above that ye are able; but with the temptation will also make a way to escape that you may be able to bear it." (1st Corinthians 10:13)

CHAPTER FIVE
STAND, PRESS AND FORGIVE

"But what things were gain to me, those I counted loss for Christ." (Philippians 3:7)

As God began to draw me closer in even a deeper walk with him and defining the mandate for my life, he began to strip me even more. However, this time it was a little different, and at times it felt harsh. He began to strip away relationships, starting with the ones nearest to me, family, friends, acquaintance and associates. Some who, at one point in my life, I wanted to pattern my life after. Role models and mentors suddenly were out the door. As God began to do a new thing in me, he strategically placed people in my life to impact my life with deeper spiritual concepts and value, taking me to a higher level in his anointing.

In August 2000, I had a supernatural experience that changed my life forever, a vision of hell. In this encounter with hell, I saw ministers in hell and they were not preaching the gospel. They were repenting and crying out to the Lord for mercy. There was great kings there as well. I think about how the countries are going to war and how no one seems to be able to get along with anyone for any period of time, yet in hell every person there was on the same accord and they were crying out to the Lord for mercy and repenting for the things that they had done while here on Earth. It never ceases to amaze me how so many people believe there is a heaven but they do not believe that there is a hell. God put a mandate on my life to share my experience of hell and to share the plan of salvation to the world. The book, videos, cassettes and CD's on *Hell is a Real Place* are now available.

My walk with the Lord has not been a piece of cake but neither was it for Jesus. There is a price that comes along with his anointing. The Bible says, "To who much is given, much is required." (Luke 12:48) There were times when I felt like the hen in the old fairy tale, *The Little Red Hen* who planted some wheat, harvested it, threshed it, took it to the mill to be grounded into flour and make the flour into bread. Everyone she asked for help said, "Not I." When she had finished cooking the bread, the little Red Hen asked the question, "Who will help me eat the bread?" And everybody's hand went up. They responded, "Oh, I will." But the Little Red Hen replied, "Oh, no you won't; I will." And that's how I felt as I reached out to people whom I had expected would understand where I was coming from and would help me. I so desperately needed guidance being a young woman in the ministry. People I thought were with me and for me turned out to be not for me at all. Sad to say, some of the people were family members.

Joseph, the son of Jacob was loved greatly by his father. His brothers hated him and they would talk to him any kind of way. God's hands were upon Joseph's life, and they hated him even more. Joseph would share his dreams with them that the Lord had shown him and the Bible states that they hated him all the more. They conspired to kill him and put him in a pit and they made up a lie to tell their father that an evil beast devoured him. One of his brothers pled for his life, to let him live and placed him in a pit. They stripped him of his coat and sold him to a group of Ishmaelites that were passing by for twenty pieces of silver. Joseph was taken into Egypt to prison. His brothers killed a goat and dipped Joseph's coat into his blood, then returned back to their father's house with Joseph's coat in their hands telling their father that an evil beast had killed him. The book of Genesis describes the hurt and pain Joseph had to endure because of the calling upon his life. Genesis 39:2,3,6 states,

"The Lord was with him and he was a prosperous man; and he was in the house of his master, the Egyptian and his master saw that the Lord was with him and that the Lord made all that he did to prosper in his hand and that Joseph was a Godly person and well favored."

Saints of God, believe me when I tell you this, when God has a calling on your life, you have been picked out to be picked on. Joseph's first suffering of persecution came from his family. Secondly, it came from his work place (Potiphar's house) where he was falsely accused by Potiphar's wife and then thrown into prison for two years. The scriptures teach us in Matthew 10:36, "A man's foes shall be they of his own household" and Micah 7:6 says, A man's enemies are the men of his own house." However be it, Jesus declared in the sermon on the mount, "Blessed are they which are persecuted for righteousness sake; For theirs is the kingdom of heaven. Blessed are ye, when men shall revile you and persecute you and shall say all matter of evil against you falsely for my sake. Rejoice and be exceedingly glad for great is your reward in heaven; for so persecuted they the prophets which were before you." (Matthew 5: 10-12)

Like the Apostle Paul, "I learned whatever state I am, therewith to be content, willing." If you look closely at that portion of the scripture, you will see that Paul said he had to learn to be content. It did not just come spontaneously. That is why it is so painful when we are going through. The flesh does not want to die to the spirit man, it has to be taught to submit and humble to the will of God for our lives.

Joseph knew at a very young age that God was with him but Joseph still had to be taught. The anointing was being manifested in his life because of the mandate God had upon his life to save Egypt. The Lord had to allow Joseph to be broken and stripped before he could really use him. The Lord had to humble him, even though Joseph knew he possessed the gift of prophesy. He rubbed that gift into his brother's faces and they got tired of it. So, God allowed them to place Joseph into the pit and sell him. It was there that Joseph experienced brokeness and humility. He learned that although he was in a situation where he had done no wrong, he did not have to allow the situation to control his destiny. While Joseph submitted to the one that had the rule over him, he continued to allow the Lord to use him for his glory. Joseph's presence there began to change things around him. When God puts you in a place or if he allows you to be put in a place, he puts you there for a purpose, to be a light in a dark place. You have to go in and possess the land, not be overtaken by the enemy in that land. Joseph remained steadfast in his faith that the Lord was greater than his situation or any problem he had. He was faithful unto the Lord. Joseph knew in the fullness of time, his gift would make room for him and that this situation was just a temporary problem. He knew who he was in Christ Jesus, and he knew that he would someday possess the land. But first he had to endure the process of brokeness and be stripped for the master's use.

Once I realized what the Lord was doing in my life, the process got a whole lot easier. I too had to learn, as Joseph and Paul, to submit my will to the will of the Lord. This can only be done by keeping your eyes fixed and unmoved on the Lord no matter what distraction may come your way because *come your way they will*. The prophet Isaiah said, "They that wait upon the Lord, shall renew their strength. They shall mount up with wings of eagles. They shall run and not be weary. They shall walk and not faint." (Isaiah 40:30)

We also have to remember one thing in waiting on the Lord. We must be steadfast watching as well as praying, vigilant and not asleep. Paul said, "I press toward the mark of the calling. Which was in Christ Jesus." And Joseph had to learn to forgive his brothers for betraying him, though he was hurt and he missed them and his father, he chose to love them and not to hate them. I too had to choose good over evil. I had heard people say, "Following the Lord will cost you something." But I say, "Following the Lord will cost you everything."

I also realize that God is a rewarder to those who diligently seek him. There are no short cuts or quick fixes. I believe what the Lord did in biblical days, with great men and women of faith, he is doing the same thing today, stripping, shaping, molding and humbling his people of God, calling them to live a clean and holy life because, "Iron sharpeneth iron; so a man sharpeneth the countenance of his friend. And the trials of our faith is only for a season. For in due season, we will reap if we faint not."

In Luke 12:41-48, Peter required of the good servants, "Then Peter said unto him, Lord speakest thou this parable unto us or even to all? And the Lord said, who then is that faithful and wise steward whom his Lord shall make ruler over his household, to give them their portion of meat in due season? Blessed is that servant when his Lord cometh and shall find so doing. Of a truth I say unto you that he will make him ruler over all that he hath. But if that servant say in his heart my Lord delayeth his coming; and shall begin to beat the men servants and maidens and to eat and drink and to be drunken; The Lord of that servant will come in a day when he looketh not for him and at an hour when he is not aware and will cut him in sunder and will appoint him his portion with the unbelievers and that servant which knew his Lord's will, and prepared not himself, neither did according to his will, shall be beaten with many stripes for unto whosoever much is given, of him shall be much required; and to whom men have committed much of him they will ask the more."

We have to take our eyes off of family, friends, the world, relationships and things and keep our eyes on the Lord because family, friends, the world, relationships and things will cause you to go to hell. When Jesus was teaching the multitude and they all sat about him, they said unto him, "Behold, thy mother and thy brethren who seek for thee and he answered them saying, Who is my mother or my brethren? And he looked around about on them which sat about him and said, Behold my mother and my brethren! For whosoever shall do the will of God, the same is my brother and my sister and mother." (Mark 3: 31-55) "Then Peter began to say unto him, Lord, we have left all and have followed thee. And Jesus answered and said, verily I say unto you, there is no man that hath left house, or brethren, or sisters, or father, or mother, or wife, or children, or lands, for my sake and the gospel's. But he shall receive a hundredfold now in this time, houses, and brethren, and sisters, and mothers, and children, and lands, **WITH PERSECUTIONS**, and the world to come eternal life. But many that are first shall be last; and the last first." (Mark 10:28-31) It is clear that Jesus put a lot of emphasis on the kingdom of heaven, not things, nor people. What I believe he is saying to us is not to get sidetracked in all of these things, to love God with all of our hearts, and with all of our minds and souls. He will reward us, and he will sustain us. If we seek first the Kingdom of God and his righteousness, all of these things shall be added unto us. It is very important for us to remember Jesus said all these things will come with persecutions according to Mark 10:30. When we are going through and being tried by the fire, the word persecutions has an *S* at the end, which signifies *more than one*.

CHAPTER SIX
HE'S MY BROTHER

"He that loveth not his brother abideth in death." (I John 3:14)

The story of two brothers, Abel a keeper of sheep and Cain a tiller of the ground, is written according to Genesis 4:1-16. In the process of time Cain brought an offering of the fruit of the ground unto the Lord, while Abel brought an offering of the firstlings of his flock and the fat and the Lord had respect for Abel and his offering. But unto Cain and his offering he had no respect and Cain became very angry and disappointed. The Lord rebuked Cain for his attitude. He told him that sin lieth at the door. Cain became jealous of his brother Abel. Cain smooth talked Abel while luring him into the field to kill him. The Lord said unto Cain, "Where is Abel thy brother?" And he said, "I know not; Am I my brother's keeper?" The answer to that question is *yes*. We are our brother's keepers. The Lord did not give a *yes* or *no* reply. He simply asked, "What hast though done? The voice of thy brother's blood crieth unto me from the ground." The Lord, all knowing and foreknowing, already knew that Abel was dead, but he wanted to give Cain a chance to confess his sins and repent to him before he pronounced judgment upon him, but Cain did not. Cain forced the Lord's hand of judgment when he could have had mercy. The Lord said, "Now art thou cursed from the earth, which hath opened her mouth to receive thy brother's blood from thy hand? When thou tillest the ground it shall not henceforth yield unto thee her strength. A fugitive and a vagabond shalt thou be in the earth. And Cain said unto the Lord, my punishment is greater than I can bear. Behold thou hast driven me out this day from the face of the earth and from thy face shall I be hid and I shall be a fugitive and a vagabond in the earth. And it shall come to pass that everyone that findeth me shall slay me. And the Lord said unto him, Therefore whosoever slayeth Cain, vengeance shall be taken on him sevenfold. And the Lord set a mark upon Cain, lest any finding him should kill him and Cain went out of the presence of the Lord.

The Lord, plentiful in mercy, wanted Cain to repent of his sin. Cain tried to lie his way out and when he saw that would not work, he tried to justify what he had done by asking, "Am I my brother's keeper?" Finally he played his "pity card." The *poor little me* role, but grace was still there for him. The Lord did not kill him, instead he set a mark upon him to shield and protect him so no one else would kill him.

For as much as we would like to retaliate against someone who has hurt us or caused us pain, we cannot. If we are who we say that we are in Christ Jesus, the Lord requires us to continue to walk in love with our brethren – and not only love them but pray for them so that their blood will not be upon our hands. Jesus said, "Whosoever committeth sin is the servant of sin," and "If you love me, keep my commandments." (John 8:34 and John 14:14) When Jesus taught the sermon on the mount, he shared his heart with the disciples and the people. He told them many things; he was teaching them how to face and accept different challenges that were yet to come in their lives when he have been lifted up from the earth. I think one of the most important things he was trying to teach them was how to love and forgive each other. He gave them some examples to go by. He said in Matthew 5:38-45, "Ye have heard that it hath been said, an eye for an eye, and a tooth for a tooth: But I say unto you, that ye resist evil but whosoever shall smite the on thy right cheek, turn to him the other also, and whosoever shall compel thee to go a mile, go with him twain. Give to him that asketh thee and from him that would borrow of thee turn not thou away. Ye have heard that it hath been said, thou shalt love thy neighbor and hate thine enemies, but I say unto you, love your enemies, bless them that curse you, do good to them that hate you and pray for them which despitefully use you and persecute you, that ye may be the children of your father which is in heaven; for he maketh his sun to rise on the evil and on the good and sendeth rain on the just and on the unjust." Then he goes on to teach them forgiveness in the Lord's prayer – forgiveness for our debtors, for if ye do not forgive men their trespasses, neither will your father forgive your trespasses." (Matthew 6:2, 14, 15) By this we see the heart of our Father through Jesus.

Jesus wanted us to reconcile always with our brother. He is also showing us the only way that we can enter into the throne room is with a repentant heart. He said, "If you come before the altar and you have unforgiveness in your heart or aught against your brother, it does you no good to come nor to bring your gift until you have reconciled with your brother." Jesus said, "A new commandment I give unto you that ye love one another as I have loved you, that ye also love one another. By this shall all men know that ye are my disciples, if ye have love one for another."

Perhaps, if Cain had humbled himself in the sight of the Lord, his fate may have been different. Perhaps if he had not spoken evil of his brother, the Lord would have allowed him to stay in his country among his people. Perhaps if Cain had prayed and sought the Lord's face before he decided to take the law into his own hands, Able's life would not have been taken. The Bible teaches us that, "Where envying and strife is, there is confusion and every evil work." It teaches us that, "The tongue is a fire. It is unruly, evil, full of deadly poison and it cannot be tamed." But it also teaches us, "To humble yourselves in the sight of the Lord and he shall lift you up and not to speak evil of another brother."

Now, in the book of Numbers the first chapter, contention arose between Moses, his sister Miriam and his brother Aaron concerning Moses' marriage to an Ethiopian woman and concerning Moses being a prophet of God. Miriam and Aaron were jealous of Moses and they said, "Hath the Lord indeed spoken only to Moses? Hath he not spoken also by us?" And the Lord heard it. According to

Micah 6:4, the Lord declared, "For I brought thee out of the house of servants; and I sent before thee Moses, Aaron and Miriam." Exodus 15: 20-21 states that "Miriam the prophetess took a timbrel in her hand and led all the women out dancing and singing to the Lord, for he hath triumphed gloriously. The horse and his rider hath he thrown into the sea. Miriam led Aaron against Moses with her jealousy and pride. The Lord called them out and rebuked them with his anger. He caused leprosy to come upon Miriam. She became white as snow. However, Aaron was guided to repent, asking Moses for forgiveness and pleaded with him not to lay the sin upon them, crying out to Moses for mercy on behalf of himself and Miriam and asking him to intercede for them for healing for their sister Miriam. Then the Lord said to Moses, If her father had but spit in her face, should she not be shut out from the camp seven days, and after that let her be received in again. And Miriam was shut out from the camp seven days and the people journeyed not till Miriam was brought in again."

We see in this portion of the scriptures, family members as we saw with Cain and Abel. The spirit of jealousy manifested, and what happened when they touched the anointing upon the lives of those men of God? Cain became a fugitive and a vagabond driven out of his country. Miriam became a leper and was also driven out of the camp for seven days. "The good man is perished out of the earth: and there is none upright among men: they all lie in wait for blood; they hunt every man his brother with a net." (Micah 7:2) The scripture tells us that, "There is none righteous, no, not one; and all our righteousness are as filthy rags." (Romans 3:10 and Isaiah 64:6)

Nevertheless, we still have to love. Jesus did not ask us how we felt about it nor did he suggest to us how to feel about it. He *commanded* us how to feel about it – that is for us to love each other. He said to love our enemies and do good to those who hate us. Bless those that curse you, pray for those who despitefully use you. (Luke 6:27-28)

In my walk with the Lord, I had to make some painful decisions. Before I was married, I was not saved. After I was married, I became saved, filled with the Holy Ghost, called into the ministry, ordained and given a mandate from God to preach and teach on salvation and hell – while my husband still remained unsaved and serving his god. He was given a mandate from his god to make my life a living hell. Satan used him <u>big time</u>. Every chance he got, he would tear me down in words and deeds. There were times when I asked God, *Do I still have to love him?* Because he would say and do things to intentionally hurt me. However, in the process, God was doing something in me, that was bigger than both of us. He was taking me into a deeper level of the Fruits of the Spirit and the character of God, the long suffering and patience. God really had his work cut out for him on those two and the scripture that says, "Be angry but sin not." I had the "be angry" part down pat, but I was having problems with the "sin not" part. But I still had to love my husband.

I had to flood my spirit with love scriptures. I would be walking around the house quoting love scriptures to myself. I had sense enough to know, "That everyone that loveth is born of God, knoweth God" and that "God was love." And I sure did not want to be born of the devil. So I had to pray and work at loving when I did not feel like loving, when I just wanted to throw up both of my hands and walk away. I had to learn that the enemy will use people closest to you to try to destroy you, and he will supercede if you let him. I thank my Lord Jesus that "Greater is he that is in me, than he that is in the world." I know who I am in Christ Jesus. And this is the record that Jesus left on high, "If a man say, I love God and hateth his brother, he is a liar; for he that loveth not his brother whom he hath seen, how can he love God whom he hath not seen and this commandment have we from him, that he who loveth God loves his brother also."

The Bible teaches us, "If we would first judge ourselves, we should not be judged, for who are we to judge another man's servant? To his own master, he standeth or falleth. He shall be held up, for God is able to make him stand. But why dost thou judge thy brother? Or why dost thou set at nought thy brother? For we shall all stand before the judgment seat of Christ. Judge not, and ye shall not be condemned; forgive and ye shall be forgiven. How can thou say to thy brother, brother let me pull out the mote that is in thine eyes when thou thyself beholds not the beam that is in thine own eye? Thou hypocrite, cast out first the beam out of thine own eye and then shalt thou see clearly to pull the mote that is in thy brother's eye. (1st Corinthians 11:31, Romans 14:10, Luke 6:37, 42) So, despite our differences we still have to love, because our enemies are still our brothers. And we are our brother's keeper.

CHAPTER SEVEN
LORD, LET MY LIFE STAND FOR SOMETHING

"But we have this treasure in earthen vessels, that the excellency of power may be of God, and not of us." (2nd Corinthians 4:7)

Throughout the Bible, we have seen great men of God facing adversity, broken to God's will, quietly suffering as servants of God, facing one adversary after another, humbled beneath the cross as Jesus suffered silently. I see so many believers wanting to be at the top in ministries. They want a great name and they want people to look up to them but what they fail to realize is the price you have to pay to walk that close to the Lord. You may see envious, cold looks, cruel comments and silent treatment when entering a room. But what they do not see is how you have labored and laid before the Lord. They do not see the humility, the fragility and brokenness you have endured for years, the sacrifices you have made without compromising your integrity as a person, your love for the Lord in keeping his commandments, living a clean and holy life before the Lord. They see you as climbing the ladder to the top over night (and it may very well seem that way,) but it only appears that way to them because they have not stayed steadfast, vigilant and praying themselves. They have been so busy playing church, watching everybody else and minding everybody else's business until time has slipped away, leaving them standing still. They do not see or realize the price you had to pay to be where you are, all because they have been like the ant and the grasshopper. The ant works hard all summer gathering and storing food for the winter, in the hot sun all day. The ant works from sun up to sunset preparing for the long cold days ahead, while the grasshopper jumps and plays around all day in leisure, laughing at the ant, calling him foolish for not taking advantage of the warm, pretty days in the sun. The grasshopper hops and flies, bathing in the sun until the winter comes and he does not have food for the winter. When the grasshopper gets hungry, he goes to the ant to ask him for food. The ant tells the grasshopper, "You mocked and made fun of me while I was preparing for the winter, storing up food. Now you are standing there knocking at my door, wanting me to let you come into my warm house and eat up my food. No, I think not. I only have enough food to take me through the winter."

So it is that the grasshopper is left alone to die, hungry and out in the cold. As Christians, if we are not careful, we will sit on the fence until the Lord return, playing church while our souls hang in the balance. We will become spiritually dead and ultimately be left outside of the will of God to die as the grasshopper, hell bound for all eternity.

People are looking at the glitter and the gold, the prestige, the biggest house and the finest cars. They do not see the suffering servant. They do not see the loneliness at the top nor do they understand that you cannot share everything with everybody. People will try to get close to you just to use you, especially church folk and family members. They will take your kindness for weakness, and they will attach themselves to you if they think that you have money.

When we look at King David, we see him being broken to the will of God in many adversities; but the thing I like most about David is that he did not look at the magnitude of the situation. He focused his faith on God's word. When David accepted Goliath's challenge, he knew that Goliath was twice his size and twice his height; David would not allow Goliath's size to dictate to him who he was in Christ Jesus. He cried out, "Who is this uncircumcised

Philistine that should defy the armies of the living God?" Goliath, arrayed with a helmet of brass, a coat of mail, greaves of brass legs, a target of brass between his shoulders and a spear, and a man bearing a shield went before him. David was only armed with a staff in his hand, five smooth stones out of a brook in a bag and a slingshot. David told Goliath and the Philistine, "Thou comest to me with a sword and with a spear and with a shield: But I come to thee in the name of the Lord of hosts, the God of the armies of Israel, whom thou hast defied."

I believe David was tired of being at the backside of the woods with nobody to talk to or to share his dreams, ideas or thoughts. There was not a soul to be found to communicate with. However, when Samuel anointed David (and the spirit of the Lord came upon him,) a change begin to take place deep down on the inside of David. A spirit of boldness came over him and something began to be birthed within him. Though his countenance was beautiful to look upon and he was an inexperienced young man in war, he was no longer satisfied being a sheep keeper. (Doubtless, David must have been longing for a mate as well.) When he came into the camp where his brothers were, he heard them talking about the Philistine, Goliath. Everyone was afraid of him and ran from him. They talked about the reward the king offered for killing him. David quickly decided he wanted in on it also. He realized that if he killed Goliath, it would be the answer to all of his prayers. He would be an instant millionaire. He could have the King's very own daughter for his wife, a free house, great riches and a great name to go along with it. David may have been small in stature but no one could say that David was a fool. David set his sights on killing Goliath – and kill Goliath he did. David became Saul's son-in-law but Saul deceived him time and time again. When God begins to elevate you, family members, friends and even great leaders like Saul will become your worst enemy because God is raising you up.

I believe David wanted his life to stand for something. I believe he must have said, "If I die, let it stand for something in the Lord." He had already been anointed by Samuel; he was an anointed servant of God; that is why he could go up against Goliath with just a staff, a sling and five stones. David said to the Philistine, *Though you maybe big and mighty, bring it on because with all of your armor, you are still no match for the name of the Lord!*

Though he had been called, anointed and sent of God, David still had to wait on God. He had to wait for the proper time to be elevated in authority. David started out as Saul's armor bearer and the Lord continued to use him, taking him to greater heights and deeper depths in the Lord. Just like Saul the King, the Philistine Goliath and all of the other giants in the land, we will have to face kings and giants in our walk with the Lord. Everybody that says that they are with you is not with you and we must know who the real enemies are, whether they are friends or foes.

Sometimes I stop and look back over my life, how the enemy in my home rose up against me. There were times when I wondered if God was asleep because it seemed like I was in one battle after another and Satan was whipping me pretty well. I was battling with some health problems; I was battling with my children's rebellious spirits; I was battling in my marriage with my husband's infidelity and the spirit of drug problems; I was battling with my brother and some of my sisters; I was battling with former spiritual leadership; and (last but not least,) I was battling within myself trying to stay spiritually focused on the Lord in the midst of total chaos. Sometimes the greatest battle that you are fighting is the one going on in the inside of you.

It has not been easy. There have been some disappointments, some sunshine and some rain. There have been spiritual battles, but – glory to God! – he sustained me. "He took my broken pieces and gave me a brand-new start. Jesus kept me so that I would not let go." Many people see me now and see how far the Lord has brought me, but they do not know what I have been through. They don't see the spiritual scars and wounds, the knots and bruises, the tears that I have shed and the punches that I took to stand this close to see God's glory. Struck down but not destroyed, I am more than a conqueror in Christ Jesus who strengthens me. Hallelujah to the Lamb of God!

In October 1995, the Lord called me to preach the gospel of Jesus Christ. I was in a small Baptist church that was very family oriented.

My father and mother, my grandparents and their grandparents, uncles, aunts and all of the other cousins grew up in that church. A legacy of families attending the same church for years – that type of church. A church deeply rooted in tradition, in the deep south. So when the Lord spoke to me about my calling, I knew that I was already in trouble as far as stepping forward announcing that the Lord had called me to preach. He told me I would be as John the Baptist was back in Jesus' days. I would be a forerunner for the next woman that came along in that church. In other words, the Lord already knew the outcome, he just wanted me to be obedient and step forward. He told me that I would be mocked and persecuted, but as he did for his son, so would he also do for me. He would raise me up on the third day. God even told me where he was sending me and how long it would take me to get there, but he told me that I had to stay there until the work I was sent there to do was finished.

So, step forward I did – and cut down I was. The Lord had instructed me what would take place, and he also warned me that I could not speak. I could not open my mouth in my defense and so it was that his word would be fulfilled. The night that I went before the councils, they all sat judging me. I was told to explain why I felt the Lord had called me to preach. When I did, the entire council sat still, apparently astonished at what I had said. Already with their minds made up, the Chief Council demanded for me to show him in the Bible where God used a woman to preach. He told me, "If you can show me anywhere in the scriptures where the Lord used a woman to preach the word, then I will let you preach, but if you cannot then I will not because no place in the Bible, have I read that the Lord used a woman to preach the word." My heart was crushed even thou the Lord had told me what would take place. Nothing could have prepared me for what I felt. Out of the multitude of councils, there was only one man that stood up to speak on my behalf. He stood three times to defend me and three times he was told to sit down by the Chief Council, rebuked for my sake. All I could do was to sit there. I never said a word. "Persecuted but not forsaken; cast down but not destroyed." I wanted to ask him, "What Bible have you been reading? Don't you know that Mary, Jesus' mother was the one who carried the word and the word became flesh and dwelt among men? Don't you understand that Mary was a woman? If God chose a woman to be a vessel to carry his son, his word, don't you think if she was good enough for God to trust the future of the world into her hands? Don't you think that it is highly possible for him to use a woman to carry the good news of the gospel?"

Throughout the bible, we see how the Lord used women to fulfill his word and how they ministered unto the Lord while he walked the face of the earth. In stillness, I sat there as tears rolled down my cheeks. I never said a word. Now, I don't know what Jesus must have felt that day when he went before all of the Chief Councils and Rulers, before they crucified him on the cross, but I am well acquainted with the suffering, the pain, the humiliation of being stripped naked in the spirit realm. I still had to love them and forgive them. I am sure that was the main reason the Lord would not release me from that church until he was certain that I harbored no bitterness and unforgiveness in my heart. What I experienced that night was so in line with what Jesus experienced before he was crucified. Yet, in the midst of it all, the Lord spoke to me that night, as I lay awake in the middle of the night. He said, "In three days, I'll raise you up." I did not know what that meant; all I knew was everything on the inside of me was hurting. I was hurt that God would tell me to do something that I could not do, and how it would hurt me. This happened on a Thursday night I'll never forget: *I said to myself I'll never go to church again!* I felt like I couldn't face the world again. When Sunday morning came, I was lying in bed and I tried to stay there, but the Lord would not let me. I tossed and turned until about 11:30 a.m. and I heard the voice of the Lord say, "Get up and go into the house of the Lord." I got up not really wanting to obey, but I submitted. I got up and got dressed and started on my way to church, and as I drove down the road, it seemed like someone else was driving the car for me. I found myself turning down a street to a church I had no intention of attending. Still I ended up pulling up into the parking lot. I sat there trying to talk myself out of going inside. But I was dealing with a force too big for me, and I was no match for God. It was about 12:45 p.m. I felt bad because it was too late to be going to church, but there was no way God was about to let me off the hook. He knew my whole walk with him was at sake if I did not face my fears. So, finally I got up the courage to go inside of the church and as I started to touch the door a usher opened the door and as he was about to take me to be seated, the pastor stopped preaching and said these words, "There you are! I've been waiting for you to come. The Lord spoke to me about you, and I was beginning to think that you were not going to show up." He continued, "Usher, bring her up here to the pulpit; she's an evangelist." I looked around wondering whom he was talking about because no one else was coming into the sanctuary at that time but me. The pastor spoke again, "I'm talking about you." I looked up at him thinking surely he must think that I am someone else, so I pointed to myself. *Who me?* He said, "Yes, I am talking about you. The Lord woke me up last night and told me about you and that you would be here today and the things you have been going through. He told me to ordain you, give you your license and put you to work. Come on up here to the pulpit anytime you are in this church. You are welcome at this pulpit." I cannot tell you what I felt. I just began to weep as he went on with his sermon. He greeted me as his brethren. This man did not know me at all. He and I had never met. As a matter of fact, he was from out of town and only came to preach at that particular church. After the service was over, the sisters of the church prepared dinner for him in the fellowship hall of the church. He invited me to have dinner with him after the service. We ate and fellowshipped together. He told me all about how the Lord had woken him up that night telling him about me, and giving him instructions.

It truly blessed me. I did not have to tell him anything about what had taken place; he already knew. The Lord did resurrect me on that Sunday, (three days later) as he said he would. However, I declined at that time to be ordained and licensed because so much of this was new to me, especially hearing the voice of the Lord; I never knew before then that the Lord would actually talk to you. So I respectfully declined with the door opened for a later time. For these reasons, I want to thank and praise God for Minister Willie Brown who was the pastor of St. John AME Church here in Eatonton, Georgia. He is a mighty, anointed man of God, who is walking closely with the Lord. My brother, I openly and publicly acknowledge you for your boldness and strength in being obedient to the Lord. I truly believe if it had not been for you on that day, I more than likely would have turned my back on the Lord, and I would not be walking with the Lord today. Again thank you and thank God for his love for saving us. May the Lord bless you, in Jesus name. Amen.

I know we all have a story to tell, a testimony of God's goodness and I thank God for this journey. I would not take anything for my journey now. So many times I am asked, "How do you know this or that?" and "I want the same gift that you have." They see me now and fruits that are being manifested; they do not see the process it took me to get me where I am, and I am by no means where God is trying to get me to. I have not arrived yet, and I pray that the Lord will always continue to shape and mold me into his image, changing me from glory to glory, until the Lord returns. Being the first ordained prophetess in ministry in a small country town in Putnam County – (I believe I was the third ordained female minister in the county – it was no piece of cake, let me tell you! Especially operating in the gift of End-Time Prophecy. That only made matters worse, because most people did not understand the Holy Spirit or the gifts of the five-fold ministry. But I praise God that the city has come along way since that time. Now there are a several more female ministers here, who are fulfilling their destiny and are called to preach the Gospel of Jesus Christ. I praise God for what he is doing and the doors that are being opened for the lady ministers.

However, I came along in a time when it was unacceptable for a woman to be a minister. It was *No, no, no, sit down and shut up. Thank you very much!* My last battle was understanding the gift that I was blessed with – being filled with the Holy Spirit, the gift of tongues, the gift of prophecy. Understanding and flowing in the gifts was another story altogether. I knew that the gifts and calling of God are without repentance but there were times in my life when I was so frustrated with my gift. I felt like it was more of a curse than a gift because I did not understand what was happening to me. Then the Lord placed into my life a very anointed man of God who operated in these gifts. I thank and praise the Lord for his grace and mercy. He planted into my path my pastor, Bishop Gus Kilgore, Jr. and his lovely wife, The Elect Lady and Assistant Pastor, Joanne Kilgore who became my mentors long before they became my spiritual leaders.

The Lord had given me a vision in the early 90's to bring all ministers and churches together for a day of fasting, praying and repentance. Bishop Kilgore was one of the twelve names that the Lord gave me to contact concerning "The Day of Repentance." I had never met him prior to calling him concerning the vision. He lived in another town about fifty miles north of the city. Yet, the Lord gave me the full name of twelve ministers in the city, six of them I had never met before nor ever seen before in my life. Bishop Kilgore embraced the vision and the Lord used him mightily throughout the course of the vision and even more on the day of repentance. He was involved in an anti-drug march in his church, fighting the war on drugs on our streets in Putnam County. In the years I have known him and his lovely wife, they have been a great encouragement to me, guiding me in my walk with the Lord, helping me to understand my calling and my gift. He has been instrumental in pushing me to be bold in the Lord and to stand firm in whatever the Lord is saying and doing, always reminding me that the Lord has called prophets to be "watchmen," to blow the trumpet and warn the people of what is coming and that we have a responsibility in a sense that no other part of the body of Christ has – and if we fail to warn the people of what is about to take place, then their blood is upon our hands. Ezekiel 33:3-6 declares concerning the watchman, "If when he seeth the sword come upon the land, he blow the trumpet and warn the people; then whosoever heareth the sound of the trumpet and taketh not warning; if the sword come and take him away, his blood shall be upon his own head. He heard the sound of the trumpet and took not warning; his blood shall be upon him. But he that taketh warning shall deliver his soul. But if the watchman see the sword come, and blow not the trumpet, and the people be not warned; if the sword come, and take any person from among them, he is taken away in his iniquity; but his blood will I require at the watchman's hand." And he had taught me we must take a stand for what is right in the eyes of the Lord, no matter who it hurts. Yet, at the same time I must use wisdom and walk in love because if we fail the Lord, then we have failed them all.

The Lord used a sweet little mother in our church to instill some valuable words of wisdom into me. I was going through so much and just being shredded to pieces by different ministers and the general public concerning a vision I had on hell – the Lord had given me a mandate to preach and teach the message on salvation and hell, to warn the people that hell is a real place. She told me, "Sister West, let me tell you something, if the Lord had shown you something and has told you what to do, then I advise you to do whatever he told you to do. I am going to tell you just like he told Ezekiel, you tell them whether they will hear you or not and you will be doing what the Lord has told you to do. Don't worry about it after that. Leave it in the hands of the Lord and he will do the rest." I was so richly blessed by what that dear, precious, sweet woman of God told me. It has stayed with me until this very day and I just want to thank and acknowledge her for that seed she sowed into my life that day. I'll never forget her for that and always love her for those great words of wisdom. Her name is Mother Jessie Pearl Henderson who lives in Eatonton, Georgia. She is a great and faithful woman of God, full of wisdom beyond her years.

I went back to Ezekiel chapter three. That chapter says in verses 17-21, "Son of Man, I have made thee a watchman unto the house of Israel; therefore hear the word at my mouth, and give them warning from me. When I say unto the wicked, thou shalt surely die; and thou givest him not warning, nor speakest to warn the wicked man shall die in his iniquity but his blood will I require at thine hand. Yet, if thou warn the wicked and he turn not from his wickedness nor from his wicked ways, he shall die in his wicked ways, he shall die in his iniquity; but thou hast delivered thy soul. Again, when a righteous man doth turn from his righteousness, and commit iniquity, and I lay a stumbling block before him, he shall die; because thou hast not given him warning. He shall die in his sin, and his righteousness which he hath done shall not be remembered; but his blood will I require at thine hand. Nevertheless, if thou warn the righteous man, that the righteous sin not, and he doth not sin, he shall surely live, because he is warned; also thou hast delivered thy soul." When I got the complete revelation of what the spirit of the Lord was saying to me about my obligation to warn his people, nothing and nobody could stop me or talk me out of what I must do. Oh, it was on then! I said, *Devil, bring it on. Devil, take your best shot!*

When Ezekiel was told to eat the roll in Ezekiel 2:4-10 to Ezekiel 3:1-4, the Lord was telling him to go into the house of Israel, his chosen people, the Church, a remnant people. These were suppose to be people who knew the Lord. Yet, the Lord told Ezekiel they were a rebellious nation, a stiff-necked people, and an impudent and hard-hearted people. He declared, "For they are impudent children and stiff hearted. I do send thee unto them; and thou shalt say unto them, thus saith the Lord God and they, whether they will hear or whether they will forbear, for they are a rebellious house. Yet, they shall know that there hath been a prophet among them and thou, son of Man, be not afraid of them, neither be afraid of their words. Though briars and thorns be with thee, and thou dost dwell among scorpions. Be not afraid of their words, nor be dismayed at their looks, though they be a rebellious house and thou shalt speak my words unto them, whether they will hear, or whether they will forbear; for they are most rebellious. But thou, Son of Man, hear what I say unto thee; Be not thou rebellious like that rebellious house. Open thy mouth and eat that I give thee. And when I looked, behold an hand was sent unto me; and lo, a roll of a book was therein; And he spread it before me; and it was written within and without and there was written therein lamentations and mourning and woe, moreover he said unto thou findest, eat this roll and go speak unto the hours of Israel. So, I opened my mouth and he caused me to eat that roll and he said unto me, Son of Man, cause thy belly to eat and fill thy bowels with this roll that I give thee. Then did I eat it; and it was in my mouth as honey for sweetness. And he said unto me, Son of Man, go, get thee unto the house of Israel and speak with my words unto them. For thou are not sent to a people of a strange speech and of an hard language but to the house of Israel." Church folks who said they knew the Lord were the ones Ezekiel was first sent to warn, who had rebelled and transgressed against the Lord, even unto this day.

As the Lord sent Ezekiel before the people in full boldness of the Lord, he told Ezekiel to eat the whole roll, to tell them the whole truth, not to sugar coat it, to call a demon a demon and not be afraid of the Pharisees and the Sadducees nor the giants in the land. He said tell them because these people I have sent you to, they do not have a strange speech or a hard language and they can understand. He said they can understand, but it is up to them to believe and receive what the spirit of the Lord is saying to the Church. He is talking about stirring them up, awakening them to the warning so none would perish and none would have an excuse to be lost. There are times in our walk with the Lord when we have to choose between a relationship or God – and accept the consequences of whatever takes place thereafter, be willing to be laughed at, to be talked about and to be called crazy. However, you'd better know when a thing is not in line with the word of God. Know when something is built upon the word of God and have God as its foundation. I once heard a pastor called some of his ex-members, "Renegade Christians," saying that they were not rooted or grounded in his church. A lot of enthusiasm was placed upon "his church." Now Webster's defines renegade as a deserter of a cause. So that means somewhere in between, there had to have been some contention to cause the members' separation to take place. The scripture tells us, "Curse not the King, no not in thy thought, and curse not the rich in thy bedchamber; for a bird of the air shall carry the voice and that which hath wings shall tell the matter. Let us hear the conclusion of the whole matter. Fear God and keep his commandments for this is the whole duty of man. For God shall bring every work into judgment, with every secret thing, whether it be good or whether it be evil. For vanity is an evil disease and vanity and a vexation spirit will not profit under the sun." (Ecclesiastes 10:20, 12:13 - 14, 6:2 and 2:11) We have to be so careful as men and women of God of what we say, how we say it and to whom we say it. Sometimes our mouth can write a check that we cannot cash – and the only thing that can straighten the mess out that we have made is true repentance. We can wound people and not realize the blood we

54

have on our hands. Nevertheless, God called us to love and not hate, to forgive and not accuse. I love it the way John breaks it down to us in 1st John 3:14, "We know that we have passed from death unto life, because we love the brethren. He that loveth not his brother abideth in death and whosoever hateth his brother is a murderer; and ye know that no murderer hath eternal life abiding in him." That is so powerful to me and that keeps me on the right road, letting me know I cannot afford to error – but if I do, I cannot afford to stay in error. We all have made errors in judgment.

When James wrote to the church concerning faith and works he said in James 1:2, 3, "My brethren, count it all joy when we fall into divers temptations knowing this, that the trying of your faith worketh patience." James was not talking about falling down; James was talking about getting up to the glory of God. A great songwriter wrote, "We fall down but we get up." That's what James is talking about here. When we miss the mark (as it is for certain we will do,) repent (get up) and go on with the Lord – for the word of God declares, "And ye shall know the truth and the truth shall make you free." The only way that we will ever get free of whatever has us in bondage is by first admitting or confessing the truth, for it is the word of God that washes us and cleanses us from all unrighteousness. John 17:17, "Sanctify them through thy truth: thy word is truth." I thank and praise God for the Holy Spirit, who teaches and guides us into all truth and brings all things back to our remembrance.

Even today when I look at myself (and I see all of my imperfections and flaws,) I thank the Lord for allowing persecution to come to me, for if it had not came, God could not have built godly character in me. It has shaped me into someone I am proud to be. It has strengthened and pushed me when I wanted to give up. It has worked patience and an unwavering faith in the Lord. Joseph said, "But as for you thought evil against me, but God meant it unto good, to bring to pass, as it is this day, to save much people alive." I now know that when persecution comes, I am in the will of God.

I thank God for real men and women of God, who lay before the Lord laboring to hear from him and walking in his statues and keeping his commandments, living clean and holy lives before

God and man. Today we see many preachers standing in the pulpit confessing that they know God, but if you examine closely their lives you will find that they are unclean. Some are committing adultery in the very house of God, fathering children outside of their marriage. Some are homosexual and lesbian laying up with other men and women. Some are chasing after young teenage girls and boys. Some are robbing God, and manipulating the sheep for material gain. We see witchcraft and spiritual blackmail. We see the gifts of the Holy Spirit prostituted; we see greed and ungodly fame. We see hatred being preached from the very pulpit. The people of God are literally being crucified and stoned in the house of God, while the Jezebel Spirit is alive and well. Yet many have not discerned her activities nor her power. This demonic spirit has gained power and access into some of the lives of men and women of God who were at one time walking very closely with God and now have been deceived and blinded by greed, stupidity and the work of the flesh. Jesus said (according to Luke 9:62,) "No man having put his hand to the plough and looking back is fit for the Kingdom of God. The Epistle of Jude 4 we found these words recorded, for there are certain men crept in unawares, who were before of old ordained to this condemnation, ungodly men, turning the grace of our God into lasciviousness and denying the only Lord God, and our Lord Jesus Christ. I will therefore put you in remembrance, though ye once knew this, how that the Lord having saved the people out of the land of Egypt, afterward destroyed them that believeth not."

I received a phone call one night from a minister whom I had never met before. This minister from Birmingham, Alabama told me he had heard of my testimony of hell. He wanted to inquire about my experience. He later informed me that he had backslidden, he was no longer preaching and he did not attend church. He said that he was a car and computer software salesman. His marriage was in trouble, because he loved to chase after women. He loved to go to the shopping mall and watch and meet women. He would lie to them, saying that he was not married and did not have children. He informed me that his wife was saved, was a spirit filled believer and was praying for him. He told me that hearing my testimony of hell

56

shook him, and the spirit of God had been pulling on his heart, but he had not repented. One of the questions he asked me was, *Did you see any preachers in hell?* My answer to him was, *Yes, there were preachers in hell.*

There was a sigh, then complete silence. After taking a long, deep breath, he said, "Will you pray for me? But before you do I want to ask you one more question."

"Okay. What's your question?"

"Do you ever feel like turning back and if you do, how do you deal with it?"

I told him that this walk with the Lord is a daily walk, and daily I have to discipline myself so that I do not allow my flesh to tell me what to do. I tell it what to do.

I reminded him what Galatians 6:16, 24, and 25 says, "That if we walk in the spirit, we shall not fulfill the lust of the flesh, they that are Christ's have crucified the flesh with the affections and lusts, for if we live in the spirit, let us also walk in the spirit." That's how I stay saved by standing on the word of God, and on my knees, because I know that hell is a real place." We have to watch as well as pray. Jesus told Simon, "Satan, hath desired to have you, that he may sift you as wheat, but I have prayed for you that thy faith fail you not." I told him when he is weak, flee temptation and pray; and when he prayed, he should tell the Lord about his weaknesses, and ask him to help him to overcome them.

We have to realize that the Lord knew the temptation was going to come when he told us to pray. "Lead us not into temptation, but deliver us from evil." (Luke 11:4) It is better to never know the way than to have known it and turned away. The Bible tells us that, "The last state of man is worse than the first." (Luke 11:26) I prayed for that preacher and he gave his life back to the Lord. It really blessed me to see the Lord at work – to see the Lord do what he said he would do. We have to realize it's not about us, but it's all about what God wants to do through us. My vision of hell helped me to stay on the right road as well.

So many have testified about how their lives have been changed because of my obedience in sharing my testimony with them. So many have confessed Jesus Christ as their personal Savior and now are living for God as a direct result of that testimony until I have stopped counting the testimonies and I just thank and praise God for allowing me to be a vessel fit for the master use. I give him praises and honor! To God be all the Glory! I think the most amazing and incredible moment of my life was about six months ago when I met a young man at a gas pump, I never knew him before that day, however he recognizing me on the video *Hell is a Real Place*. (He had seen it while he was in prison somewhere in the state of Georgia.) He told me that the video had a very profound effect on his life. He is now saved and has completely turned his life around. He said he was twenty-six years old, and before he went to prison he had nothing to show for his life. He was associated with drugs, and he said after he had seen the video it had changed his way of thinking and he made God a promise that once he was a free man, he would not live that way again. He said, "Since I have been out, I have gotten me a job, I work everyday and I am not associated with drugs anymore. I go to church, and I don't do the things I used to do. My friends can't believe how I've changed. They want to know what have happened to me, and I tell them about your video; I tell them that's what happened to me. I don't want to go to hell, and ever since that day I've been straight." That young man hugged my neck and told me, "Thank you."

My heart just swelled up on the inside of me, as he quietly got into his car and drove away. I got into my car and sat there for a moment before I went on home. There is no amount of money that could have bought what I felt inside. If that whole experience had been only for that one young man, then everything I had experienced has not been in vain. That's one soul that was worth it. I was driving down the road and realized how dirty and sweaty I was. I had been helping my nephew move into his apartment that day. Suddenly, I realized how unpleasant I smelled, and I said to myself, *I know that young man had to have smelt me.* Then the Lord said, "That young man did not care what you smelt like, he only wanted to thank you for leading him to me." God does not care what we look like or smell like – he just wants us to come to him like we are, and he'll clean us up. It truly blessed me that day to see God at work.

God did not anoint me with the gift of healing, though I know it belongs to us all and we receive it by faith and we all possess the gift of healing inside of us. As much as I would like to see people healed and set free from all sickness and disease, I do not possess this gift. I like seeing them receive the gift of salvation, because with the gift of salvation comes healing, prosperity, deliverance, joy, peace and the Holy Ghost. Salvation is a package and all of these things belong to the born again believer. This young man so impacted my life that day and encouraged me to stay the course and continue to fight the good fight of faith and I want to say, "Thank you!" to this young man for sharing his testimony with me. On the days when I have to reach deep, deep down inside of me to stir up the gifts, the Lord brings people like this man to mind. Thank you wherever you are!

In all the fights and struggles, the most painful ones were those that I was fighting in my home and in my marriage – the betrayal, the adulteries, the loneliness and the unsupportive husband (morally, spiritually, mentally, financially or emotionally.) He was a man who wanted to stay young. He ran with the young crowd and enjoyed the nightlife. He stayed out late most every night. On some weekends he never came home at all and when he finally showed up, he was broke. He had blown his whole paycheck. He did not even have gas money to go to work, no money to pay the bills or support his family. Yet, I tell you I was not a saint when I married my husband. It was so hard staying saved, living in an unequally yoked marriage.

When we married, we both were unsaved, partying hard every weekend, seeing and dating other people – the whole nine yards. However, I never used drugs. The good Lord sheltered me from that, and I thank him. The nightclubs and all, we both had that in common. Then one day the Lord saved me, turned my life around and I started living for the Lord. In the meantime, my husband kept right on serving his gods joyfully – and there was many. As I cried out to the Lord to save him, he laughed at me saying that I was not a true Christian, and he would always find faults in everything that I did in order to make excuses for what he was doing. He continued to curse and play games in order to manipulate so he could get what he wanted. He often told his family and friends that the only thing I wanted from him was money and that I was too lazy to work to help him pay the bills. I can remember so very vividly when I had completed the making of the *Hell is a Real Place* video, he said, "You will never get anymore money from me. You said God told you to make the video. Well, God did not tell me, and I am not paying for it. If God wants you to make it, well, I am going to see if God is going to pay for it. You're just trying to be famous." Bless God, God did pay for them and the CDs and cassettes. Hallelujah!! Now I am believing God to pay for this book that is in the works.

My husband reminds me of Job's wife when Job was going through his trials and tribulations how Satan came to Job, through the one that was closest to him. "Then said his wife unto him, "Dost thou still retain thine integrity? Curse God and die." (Job 2:9) Surely that must have done something to Job on the inside. Nevertheless, Job stood firm in his faith and spoke to her and said, "Thou speakest as a foolish woman." Job fought the fight and he kept the faith.

I know whom I am fighting. It is not my husband, it's a spirit, a demonic spirit; it is Satan. The scripture is clear. It says that Satan walks to and fro in the earth seeking whom he may devour but Job 1:22 recorded, "In all this Job sinned not, nor charged God foolishly." As I look at my husband's betrayal, I first look at the betrayal of his covenant with God, when he broke his oath, his promise and his commitment to this marriage. I cannot control what he does or whom he does it with; I can only control how I react to it. The Lord gave me that scripture one night as I was praying for him, (after I had gotten an, "I miss you" card from one of his lovers.) The Lord said, "Whatever he does unto you, he has already done it unto me." He said, "Who then is that faithful and wise steward, whom his Lord shall make ruler over his household, to give them their portion of meat in due season? Blessed is that servant, whom his Lord when he cometh shall find so doing." (Matthew 24: 45-46) The Lord was acknowledging my pain and the hurt that I was feeling. He saw the struggles I had keeping a roof over my head and food on the table. I cried out to God about how tired I was of living like that and in those

60

verses of scriptures, the Lord reassured me that if I kept the faith, in due season, he would reward me.

So many people believe that I had made money from selling the videos, tapes and CDs of *Hell is a Real Place*. But I would like for the truth to be known. It has taken my whole life savings to complete that project. I did not do the recording of those tapes to profit; I did it to be obedient to the Lord and to win souls for the Kingdom of God. It is not about the money. It is all about souls, and if I have helped to bring just one lost soul into the Kingdom of God, then I have accomplished what the Lord predestined for me to do. I do believe that someday God is going to reward me for my faithfulness whether it be here on earth or in heaven. It really doesn't matter. All that really matters is that God's will be fulfilled in my life and I remain obedient to his word.

I am trying to get to heaven. I don't have time for foolishness. I am concerned about where I am going to spend eternity because my eyes have seen the glory of the Lord and they have seen hell with its demons and the lake of fire. I have chosen heaven to be my eternal home and not hell.

I do not want my life to be in vain. I so often cry out to the Lord to help me and strengthen me to stay on the right road. One Saturday at our church picnic, I was sitting down by the lake watching the water and the Lord begin to speak through two ravens. The first raven flew over the lake in search of prey; he flew low over the water watching for fishes in the lake. As he began his descent, he used his body as a speeding missile to dive into the water to catch the fish with his beak but he missed and had to quickly pull back up out of the water before he went head first in the lake. This raven made several attempts but to no avail. Then within a matter of minutes, along came another raven. This one was wiser than the first one. This one must had been studying the eagle technique because he came in with the swing and swiftness of the talon technique of the eagle, perfect and precise and never missing a beat. He caught the fish. When the first raven observed the second raven from afar, he quickly returned to where the fish had been caught. He even tried unsuccessfully to take the fish from the second raven, which had caught it. As they flew out of sight, I thought to myself, that is just how some Christians act. They do not want to take the time to study the word of God for themselves, they want someone else to do all of the work of studying – and feed them the word – but they want to enjoy the rewards and promises of God's benefits without the work. They want to eat from the Lamb's table of life, but they do not want to bring anything to the table.

They remind me of the ten virgins who went forth to meet the bridegroom. Five of them were wise and five were foolish. The five foolish virgins took their lamps but they did not take any oil. The five wise virgins took extra oil in their vessels and their lamps. While the bridegroom tarried, the five foolish virgins ran out of oil. They tried to get oil for their lamps from the five wise virgins. They told them, "No. We only have enough for ourselves. Go and buy some more oil for yourselves." But while they went to buy more oil, there went out a cry at midnight saying, "Behold, the Bridegroom cometh; go ye out to meet him." The five wise virgins were ready. They went in with him to the marriage and the door was shut. When the five foolish virgins returned, they called out to the Lord to open the door and let them in, but he answered and said, "Verily I say unto you, I know you not. Watch therefore, for ye know neither the day nor the hour wherein the Son of Man cometh." (Matthew 25:1-13)

We have become a complacent generation, satisfied with the crumbs on the floor rather than the pie on the table. Satisfied with the remnant of what could have been instead of walking in the blessing and the possession of our inheritance. Our minds have become too shallow in understanding who we are in Christ. Our souls have been vandalized by the world's order for today, and our spirits have been ravished by every satanic plague ever recorded in the Bible. Still, Satan cannot silence our cries before the Lamb of God. As I sat quietly facing the lake, watching the waves ripple across the water, (thinking silently to myself about all of the cares of the world,) the Lord spoke and said, "Every drop of water is mine and every grain of sand is mine. I have commanded the oceans, the rivers and the lakes to contain the waters and the earth to hold the land. Is it too much for me to ordain and order all of your affairs? As the water covers the earth (and not one drop moves out of it's boundaries, but flows from shore to shore and is subject to my command,) so shall my word go forward and it shall not return unto me void. It shall accomplish what I say. For a little while you must endure, as the trees, flowers and grass must bear the heat of the sun everyday. Do I not give them the stars and moon to them at night, a lesser light to rest from the burden of the heat from the sun during the day; with the dew to refresh and revive them for the next day?" He said, "I strengthen and condition them through the heat, the cold, the wind, the rain and the storm. I am in control of all things and their lives and if I care so much for them. How much more do I care for you?" It was 2:00 p.m.

I began to think of the multitudes of trees, plants and every blade of grass, the amount of water in the oceans and how God spoke and not one drop passed beyond its boundaries. Not one tree, plant or blade of grass goes unnoticed nor without nourishment to grow. Who am I that God cannot cause everything that concerns me to obey his word? I am reminded of how Jesus spoke to the storm and the wind and it obeyed. God spoke creation into existence and it was, and now is. I have that same creative power and authority within me to speak – and it shall be. Truly it is well with my soul. To God be all the glory.

Isaiah 55:10,11 record these words, "As the rain and snow come down from heaven and stay upon the ground to water the earth and cause the grain to grow and produce seed for the farmer and bread for the hungry. So also is my word. I send it out and it always produces fruit. It shall accomplish all I want it to and prosper everywhere I send it." (TLB) Then I noticed the fish, how playful they were – how they jumped up out of the water, how they were not concerned about the ravens, nor the needs for their lives. They totally trusted God to supply all of their needs and to shield and protect them. I realized that same God who watched over them was watching over me as well.

It had been weeks that I cried out to the Lord, *Lord show me your glory*. I was in a dry season, in a wilderness of sorts, and the Lord seemed to be very quiet. I cried out again, *Lord show me your glory* and immediately the sun went behind the clouds. In only seconds, the sun was completely covered, hidden behind the clouds. The whole sky became overcast as the new light of a white fog fell softly down to the water, which appeared to be a distance of 100 yards. The sun's rays shone from behind the clouds as if the Lord himself was descended out of the clouds.

I noticed the water had changed from a muddy dark brownish/gray to a crystal clear diamond sparkling color that was breathtaking. In the middle, there were three whirlpools. From one end of the lake to the middle, they were dancing, turning in a counter clockwise motion. What was so strange about it was that the ripples were flowing upstream, not downstream. Then I noticed trailing behind them was a fourth whirlpool. I said Lord, "What is this?" I knew even before I asked the Lord the question, what the three had to be: The Father, The Son and The Holy Ghost. But I had no idea what the fourth one was.

The Lord said that it is the Church (The Saints of God) following him.

"Wow!" I said, looking at these three whirlpools as they were right behind each other, following very closely – but the third one appeared to have a tail behind it and there was a great distance between the first three and the fourth one. As I sat there watching in astonishment, they traveled to the center of the lake and suddenly they were translated up into the rays of the sun into the sky.

It all happened so quickly. I wanted to jump up out of my chair and run back up to the province and tell the Bishop and the church members to look out over the lake. It looked like Jesus was returning! But a force held me back in my chair and I was not able to move. (It was 4:00 p.m. by this time.) Though this only lasted a matter of minutes, the glory was still in the sky. As I listened to the people laughing and talking behind me in the background – the sounds of children playing, the sounds of the iron of the horseshoes hitting together as the brothers played their hearts out. No one seemed to notice what God was doing. It made me kind of sad to know just how easily we can miss God. He is forever so close to us and we don't even notice his presence.

Suddenly I looked up when I noticed that the sound of a motorboat shut off. It was a boat that had stopped, sitting in the middle of the lake where the rays were coming from. It reminded me of a scene I had seemed in the movie, *On Golden Pond*. I noticed this boat just sat there for a while. I began to wonder if the people had been raptured away, as I did not see them and could not hear the sounds of the engines roaring. The boat began to flow slowly downstream and I was then able to see the image of the people sitting in the boat once again. However, I still could not hear the sound of the motor roaring. When the boat got to the end of the area where the rays stopped, immediately the engine started back up.

I do not know if this had anything to do with that or not, or if anything actually took place with the people in the boat. I believe it was something about being within the boundaries of that atmosphere.

It was now 4:45 p.m. at that point. I had sat there watching and waiting in God's presence. I waited on him; I paid close attention to the waves in particular to see if the same thing would take place again. As hard as I watched and waited, it did not reoccur again. The boats came and they went, both large and small, but with none effect. The whirlpool was as pure silver, as if it was liquefied. I'd never seen anything like it in all my days, and I probably will never see it ever again. But that day when Moses cried out to God, *Lord, show me your glory*. It was not God's appearance Moses wanted to see, it was the character of God he wanted to know. Moses wanted to know him personally. He wanted a closer and deeper walk with the Lord. Moses was not seeking for God to so much deliver him at that particular time, he just wanted to know and be assured that the Lord had not left him and he was still there for him. God did just that. He showed Moses just enough of his glory to assure him. *Yes, Moses I am still with you.*

God assured him of his presence.

In the middle of total destruction, hurt and pain, I still loved my husband. I guess there will always be a part of me that will forever love him. Perhaps there will always be a special bond that will tie us together. Nevertheless, I have so many questions locked inside of me. How do you tell your heart to beat again when you have lost your best friend? How do you move on and love again, and forgive the sins of the one you loved the most who has hurt you the most?

In my mind, I have a visual of cupid shooting the arrow of love in his hands into our hearts, and we fall in love all over again. I have asked God about the revelation of this and he replied, "You will love again." I know that God will heal, and I know that love will find a way. I do not doubt God, but my question to cupid is, "How can a broken arrow shoot?" Perhaps the answer is *time*, or perhaps it is in God's perfect timing. All I know to do is to trust God and wait patiently on him.

CHAPTER EIGHT
DARKNESS BEFORE THE DAWN

"Why seek ye the living among the dead? He is not here, but risen." (Luke 24: 5-6)

On March 15, 1974, the Lord blessed me with my first born, a son, John Antonio Clements. He weighed 7 lbs. 6 oz. He was a hairy little fellow, bright eyed and full of life. He was screaming and crying as if he was making an announcement to the world, "I'm here." He was wise beyond his years, and he loved to be around people older than he. He had a witty personality. He was very serious about life and wanted to make his place in the world. He was full of curiosity; and he saw life as a challenge. He loved sports, traveling and children. He also had a strong personality, and always spoke what was on his mind.

On August 28, 1994, a vibrant life ended in a head on collision. He went to be with the Lord at the scene of the accident.

Suddenly my life was changed from one level of faith to another. I remember crying out to the Lord saying, "Lord, help me, help me." I could not even pray articulately. All I could do was to call upon the name of the Lord. I begin to tell him, "Lord, you are going to have to do this because I can't." The first night I was basically in shock, and I do not remember very much except how I was hurting. I cannot explain it; if you have never lost a child, you won't even begin to understand the feeling. It is like no other loss I have ever experienced. I had recently lost my mother and father – all within the last 18 months. Just as the healing had begun, along came the death of my son, John. It hit me like a ton of bricks. I had cried so much until the tears rolled down my face, uncontrollably.

Lying across my bed, my tears streamed across my face onto the bedspread as I lay there with my eyes closed. Perhaps you did not know that you can cry with your eyes closed, but you can.

Suddenly I felt such warmth go up and down my body as I lay on my stomach. It was a continuous heat as if it were massaging my entire body. All I could focus on was the accident and my son.

I remember it as if it was yesterday. It was around 4:30 p.m. on a summer afternoon. I was standing in my front yard talking with my sister who lived in another town. She was about to leave when we heard all types of sirens. They sounded like they were blowing every type of horn they had. The neighbor's dogs began to howl with such a cry until I knew within my soul that something awful had happened. I felt a very strong prompting in my spirit to pray. I began to take authority over it and pled the blood of Jesus over the situation. I said, "Lord, somebody is in trouble. Go with them and be with them. Cover them with the blood of Jesus and have mercy on them." My sister agreed with me as we stood there staring in the direction of the sirens, not knowing that we were praying for my own son.

My sister and I finished saying our good-byes and she left. I felt something strange in my spirit and in the pit of my stomach. This was a feeling that I could not shake. As I was walking up the steps, the dogs began to howl again with a different cry than before. This sound that they were making sounded more like mourning than howling. It made me feel like I wanted to cry. In the distance, I could hear the sound of the sirens start again. As the sounds grew closer and closer the more the dogs made a mournful sound. I stopped in my tracks, listening to the sirens. I stood still as a wave of cold chills went over my body. I could not explain it, but something deep down on the inside of me would not give me peace. I stood there until I could not hear the sound of the sirens any longer and as they faded away in the distance, the dogs gradually stopped their mourning. I said to myself, "Well Lord, be with whomever that is."

When I got back into the house, I realized that it was time for me to go pick up my husband. I called my youngest son and told him it was time to go pick him up from work. It was now about 5:00 p.m. We had to wait there for him about two hours before his truck finally pulled in. When he arrived, he had a funny look on his face. He had heard on his truck CB about the wreck, and it was believed that John was one of the people involved in the accident. However, he did not tell me, because what came over the radio was that it was such a bad accident that traffic was backed up so and no one could get through. He told me to go the back way home, which was the longest way home. I wondered why we was going that way, but really did not give it much thought. After we got home, he told me to leave the car running that he had to run back to town to go to the store to pick up a pack of cigarettes. What he was really doing was going to see if John was really involved.

I said okay, still not knowing what was going on. I walked around the house to take in the laundry off the clothesline, while my youngest son went straight to the riding lawnmower to start cutting the grass.

It seemed as though I had only gotten a few pieces off of the clothesline when I heard our car horn blowing loudly. It was my husband returning home. He did not stop the car under the car porch. He drove it straight through the carport and into the backyard, still blowing the horn like somebody crazy. I was startled at his behavior. I just stood there, wondering what in the world was wrong with him. At first I thought that he was trying to get my attention because my son was making a lot of noise cutting the grass. Then he drove all the way to the clothesline, he got out of the car and said, "Come go with me, we got to go to the hospital. "John's been in an accident and we need to get to the hospital right away," he said.

I was unusually calm for some reason. I picked up the clothes basket and started into the house.

He said, "Come on! Hurry up! Leave the basket there; we don't have time for all that!" I hurriedly went into the house, changed my skirt and locked up the house, when I noticed what a mess the house was. My daughter had left her dinner untouched on the table and food was sitting in places where I did not allow food. This was not like my daughter. I hurried to the car and my youngest son said, "Mama, what the matter? Where are you all going?" I explained to him that his brother had been in an accident and we were going to the hospital to see about him.

He asked, "Can I go with you?"

I said, "Yes," and we were off to the hospital.

On the way there, we met a wrecker that was pulling a small red pick-up truck, and my flesh began to crawl. I knew from the look of the truck that it had hit something head on (and it was a known fact that most people do not walk away from a head on collisions.) I remember thinking to myself, "I hope whoever that was in that truck is all right, because it's messed up really bad." We drove on down the road a little bit further and we met another wrecker and it was pulling my son's jeep. Everyone in the car got very quiet. I felt like I couldn't move, I couldn't speak and I felt paralyzed all over and even my vocal chords seemed to be paralyzed.

My youngest son said, "Mama, that look like Tony's jeep."

I said, "It is." Suddenly, I got weak all over. I could hardly catch my breath. I keep saying to myself, *He is all right, he is all right, to comfort myself.* Deep down in the pit of my stomach, I knew that everything was not all right. I knew because of the way that both of the vehicles looked. My gut instinct was that somebody did not make it. I knew that "if" John had made it out alive, it would be a miracle. If he was alive, I knew that he had to be in really bad shape. All I could say was, *In the Name of Jesus, in the Name of Jesus.* I could not even pray.

Words would not come out of me. My mind could not form sentences. Scriptures laid dominant in me, yet, visions flooded my mind of the entire accident, like the wind blowing the pages of a book in my mind. Despite all the word of God I had inside of me, I felt totally and completely helpless.

I began to suddenly have flashbacks of a vision that the Lord had shown me about a month prior. I'd seen a really bad automobile

70

accident involving two trucks. The trucks both appeared to have been totaled. The location appeared to be coming up to a red light because I saw multi-lanes going in the same direction. I saw a tall, slim, black man's body lying in the lanes on the highway. I saw a white tennis shoe of a man lying beside the road – like on the shoulder of the road but not in the grass. I saw an ambulance parked in the middle of the multi-lanes, and I saw two men kneeling down beside this tall, slim, black man's body, placing it into a black body bag, zipping it up. I knew he was already dead. I did not see any other people. I saw white lines drawn in the road where the accident had occurred and there was such a feeling of great sorrow and pain, so much sadness and a sense of loss associated with the vision. I knew in my spirit how the Lord had always shown me things in visions and how (with every vision) came a sense of joy, sadness or pain.

But there was something especially troublesome about this one. I knew that it was someone close to me. However, God in all his mercy did not allow me to identify my son in the vision – yet he was showing me exactly what was about to take place and preparing me for the days ahead when I would have so many unanswered questions. He allowed me to be there in a vision with him.

Nevertheless, I kept on casting the vision down and pleading the blood. I told my two children who lived at home about the vision. I pled with them to stay off of the bypass because it looked like where the accident was. However, it was not the bypass.

It was on Highway 44 Northeast of Eatonton. It was not coming up to a red light, it was a caution light and it was in the multi-lanes as I was shown in the vision. All of this flooded my thoughts as we approached the hospital emergency entrance. As we pulled into the emergency parking lot, I saw several police cars. We were greeted by one of the police officers who was waiting beside his car. The officer approached my husband. I never stopped walking I had only one thing on my mind – and that was my child. There was a crowd of people gathered around the emergency area and the emergency door. Beside the wall stood my daughter and her friend. I only paused long enough to question her why she did not leave me a note or something to let me know what had happened, then I kept right on walking. I remember seeing the tears in her eyes and she did not reply to my question, for she knew he was dead – and she could tell that I did not yet know. I was in pieces and I guess I needed someone to take my feelings out on. I guess I took it out on her because I kind of snapped at her. The accident had happened at 4:20 p.m. as my son was driving home from work in a neighboring county. He left work at 4:00 p.m. and twenty minutes later, only 4.2 miles from home, two lives were gone.

It was now around 7:20 p.m. that evening. No one had contacted us concerning my son's death. My husband had known when he'd returned home to get me. Three hours had gone by before I finally arrived at the hospital.

When I entered the hospital, it was like time stood still. Everyone who was talking, suddenly stopped and all eyes seemed to be on me as if they had been waiting in anticipation for my arrival. I saw my son's girlfriend sitting there among the crowd of people. I went straight to the desk window. I identified myself and informed them that my son had been in an accident, and I wanted to know if I could come back in the emergency room area where he was. I wanted to be with him.

The desk clerk had a dumbfounded look on her face, as if she did not know what to do. So she quickly turned to a gentleman and told him that I was John Clement's mother, and I wanted to come back to see him. This gentleman came to the window and told me to just have a seat and the doctor would be out to talk to me shortly. I sat down in the chair, and I tried so hard to pray. I knew whatever it was, it was not good. All kinds of thoughts were racing through my head. I said to myself, *Oh they are going to come out here and tell me how bad off he is and they want me to sign some papers to have him air lifted to another hospital where he can get better treatments than they could provide.*

As I continue to wait, I felt the very presence of evil sitting right next to me. I heard a laughter so horrible and nasty. I turned to see who was sitting beside me. I wanted to see just what was so funny. There sat a man dressed in a black suit, shirt and tie with his hands folded and locked behind his head. His hands clinched together, rocking backward and forwards, laughing this horrid laugh saying, "Ha, ha, ha, ha, ha! Oh, ha, ha, ha, ha! Your son is dead. Now look at what your God has done. He has killed your son." He began to laugh all over again. Then he said, "Your God, whom you love so very much, killed your son."

I was in such a state of shock until it took me a moment to comprehend who this was. Suddenly I realized that no one was sitting on the entire row of seats that I was sitting on. What shocked me the most was that the devil was in an all black 3-pc. suit. I have always pictured the devil as this ugly being in old dried up skin, but in fact "he" was clean shaven with neatly trimmed sideburns and a very light mustache with fair skin. He was neatly built, and he was not overweight. His body looked like it was very well taken care of. When I recognized who he was, I said, "Devil in the Name of Jesus, you are a lie. My son is not dead and you go, in the Name of Jesus." As we stared each other face to face, he smiled at me and winked his eye at me. Then he vanished like, *Gone in sixty seconds.*

I turned back around and started to pray out loud. Until this point no one would come near me. I guess no one wanted to tell me, they were all waiting for the doctor to come out to tell me. By this time a lady that worked in the Physical Therapy Department came and knelt down at my feet, took my hands and she begin to pray with me. I became quiet and just listened to the words that she was praying into my spirit. The room was filled with silence. I felt that I was on the verge of mental collapse when a lady doctor and two paramedics came out of the back of the emergency room and called for Mrs. West.

I stood up and said, "I'm Mrs. West."

"I am Doctor So and So," she said. "Can you step across the hall with me into the physical therapy department."

I said, "Yes." My heart was racing like a racehorse. My husband, children and John's girlfriend all followed. A stream of people that seemed to come out of nowhere were there.

"I want to know to whom you want your son's body released to?" she said.

I asked, "What?"

"I want to find out from you, who you want us to release your son's body to."

"Are you trying to tell me that my son is dead?"

"I am so sorry. You did not know? I thought that you already knew."

I let out a scream that could be heard down every hall in that hospital. I grabbed the first person next to me and I just yelled, "No, no, no! He is not dead!"

As time stood still, everything seemed to be in slow motion. No, nobody had told me that my son was dead but Satan had told me and he wanted to make sure that he told me first to plant bitterness, unforgiveness and hatred into my heart. He wanted me to be angry with the Lord and he wanted me to turn my back on God so that I would serve him instead. No doctor or no other person ever told me that my son was dead. I often wondered why no one ever said he was dead but today I know why, and it is because he is not dead. He is alive in the spirit, in the presence of God.

I remember as I screamed and cried out to the Lord, a soft calm voice kneeling down in front of me said, "Mrs. West, I know that you are hurting right now and there probably isn't nothing that we could say that would ease your pain but if it would be a comfort to you, I just want you to know that I was one of the paramedics on the scene of the accident." He paused, then continued, "John did not suffer; he died on impact and he probably never even knew what hit him and I am so sorry that this happened." Those words did comfort me later on but at that particular moment, no words could comfort me. I am very grateful for this young man's compassion toward my family, and it touched my heart even more that this young man was one of my former students from a high school where I used to teach. It really blessed me to know that he had turned out to be such a fine and respectful young man.

The very next voice I heard was my pastor at that particular time saying, "Let us pray." I remember him praying, but what he said, I cannot tell you. One thing I do remember his saying was that there would be some good to come out of this. As he prayed, he thanked the Lord for the "good" that would come out of this tragedy.

I recalled how I looked up at him when he said that. I felt anger rising up in me, wondering how in the world any good could come out of so much pain. I wanted to ask him how in the world any good could come out of my son being killed.

I was angry with him, but out of respect for him. I kept quiet and did not question him. However, today I am very thankful for my former pastor, because he saw what I could not see because of my pain. Let me explain how some good did come out of it.

The next thing I knew all my sisters, my brother, in-laws, etc. all crowded into this room. People were standing in the hallway outside of the room and some on the outside of the building. So we moved to the hospital chapel where it was much quieter. It was then that I was brought my son's personal belongings. Pain overwhelmed me. I guess until now, it had not hit me that he was really gone, and I cried and cried until I could not cry anymore. As I reflect back on that day, it seems to be in parts and pieces – snapshots from some movies where the family is given the deceased's personal affects.

It did not seem real, yet the pain was real – and that was no joke. What I felt was very much real. No one knows pain unless they have been made to feel it. No one knows sorrow unless they have been made to grieve, and surely no one can understand all of the burdens of afflictions that come along with it unless they have had to bear it. People say when they are trying to comfort you, "I know how you feel." But the fact is that no one knows how that person truly feels unless they have had to endure the same thing.

I was taken home. As we walked toward the car, people from everywhere were standing outside the hospital and in the parking lots to show their support. As we passed by them, it was like a receiving line. People were giving their condolences. When we finally got home, all I wanted was to be left alone but that was one thing I was not about to get. Someone was always there throughout the entire process until well after the burial. For days I could not eat, I could not sleep and I did not want to take a bath or comb my hair. I just wanted to be left alone and for all of this to just go away. A part of me died that day. These are emotions that only a mother could feel.

I felt that I had been cheated, because I was not allowed to see my son's body at the hospital. I was angry, because I did not get the chance to say good-bye. The doctor, the paramedics, the police would not allow me to go near him. One of the policemen that had worked the scene, stopped my husband in the parking lot before we entered the hospital and told him, "No matter what you do, I advise you do not allow your wife to see his body – for her sake." I did not understand why no one would allow me to see him until later on. I learned that he was unidentifiable at the scene, and he was identified only by his driver's license. They were all trying to protect me.

As time went on, I laid across my bed and all I could think about was I did not get a chance to say good-bye. I was not there to hold him in my arms and tell him that everything would be all right. He must have been so scared and alone, and I was not there when he needed me the most. I wanted to tell him how much I loved him and how proud I was that he was my son. I know that he knew this, but somehow I wanted to make his hurt all better.

I did not know how much pain he had suffered that day before the end. All of these things were very heavy on my heart and they just ate at me until I became consumed with them. This was the darkness before the dawn.

On the third day, the Lord showed up in my bedroom and when I came out of my room, I came out preaching and teaching the word according to the gospel of Matthew and Luke – "He is not here, for he is risen, why seek you the living among the dead? And the whole atmosphere changed that afternoon from mourning to worship from that day my life changed forever. No one understood what had happened to me.

I had a complete turn around, a supernatural breakthrough and no one could comprehend. From that point on, I would not allow that spirit of grief to torment me or my loved ones. Although I truly feel no one understood what had happened, they just went along with the idea to comfort me. Howbeit, seeds were planted that day and a harvest of souls has now come into the Kingdom of God. (Matthew 28:1-9 and Luke 24:1-8)

After everything was over, the Lord laid it on my heart to put together a video of my son's life and to show it, honoring him in my home. So, for that Thanksgiving, I invited all of my family over for dinner. They all accepted. I feel they did because they knew that this holiday would be very hard for me. They were not aware that I had made the video in his honor and that I would be showing it to them. I remained steadfast in my belief that the Lord had assured me that he is risen. I showed my family the video and there was not a dry eye in the entire house. Some of them had to excuse themselves to pull it together again. I think that it took some of them by surprise but by the end, everyone had returned and the Lord had done his work, the Holy Spirit moving on their hearts, preparing them for the message of salvation which the Lord had instructed me to minister to them by telling them John's testimony – how he received salvation.

This is the testimony of John A. Clements:

John had taken his girlfriend out of town for dinner and bowling. I believe that the Lord had spoken to John in that restaurant and told him that he was coming back for him and to get his house in order.

All at once while they were ordering their food, John said, "I want to go home."

She could not believe that John would be saying he wanted to go back home when they had just gotten into the restaurant and had not gotten their food. She said that John was in such a mood until she finally gave in and asked, "What is wrong with you?"

He said that he wanted to go home to his mother's house, not his house.

So she gave in and said, "All right."

They got their food to go and they left for Eatonton. On their way back, John was very quiet. While the radio was playing, she heard John crying in the background. She turned the radio down and asked him why was he crying.

"Just take me home to my mama's house," he said, but he would not tell her why.

She tried to get him to eat his food before it got cold but he would not. He just sat very still and quietly in his seat, as she drove back to Eatonton.

I believe that the home John was talking about was not an earthly home but a heavenly home. His girlfriend was unaware that he was not talking about an earthly home.

When they reached my house I heard his jeep pull up into the yard that warm summer night, and I heard his footsteps as he hurried swiftly toward the door. I could sense in his walk an urgency as I started toward the door. I immediately knew in my spirit that something was wrong even before he got to the door by the sound of the shuffling of his footsteps. I immediately got up to meet him at the door to see what was the matter. It is funny how a mother knows, even the sound of her child's walk. As I approached the door, I saw him coming up the steps. I said, "John, what's the matter?" He did not say a word, he just grabbed me around my waist, picked me up off of the floor and held me so tight that I could barely breathe and could not move. He held me so closely until he was cutting off my breath and I struggled to tell him that I could not breathe.

He was crying uncontrollably, telling me, "Mama, I love you. I love you. I love you," over and over again and I was trying to tell him I loved him every time he told me that he loved me but I could hardly get my breath. He finally let up on me enough so that I could talk to him. Still tightly embraced, I lead him back onto the front porch and we just sat looking up at a beautiful starry night.

"Mama, I love you."

I told him again that I loved him too. He laid his head on my chest like a little baby. He continued to cry bitter tears. He cried so much until my shirt was soaking wet but I did not mind. I held him in my arms as I had done so many times when he was a little boy, drying away his tears. Then I began to question him to find out what was wrong and what had brought all of this about. All he would do was to shake his head, saying "No, no, no."

I believe that the Lord was still speaking to him and he did not want to hear it. He got up and just started walking around in the front yard repeatedly saying, "No, no, no." I got up and went after him, telling him to come back, sit down and talk to me. He did but all I could get out of him was how much he loved me, his brother and sister.

"Where's my brother?"

"In the house," I told him. By that time, his youngest brother came to the door. John jumped up immediately when he heard his brother's voice, grabbed him saying, "Canvas, I love you, I love you."

His brother Canvas said, "Mama, what's John talking about? What's wrong with John?" John hugged his little brother with a great big bear hug. Saying that he loved him was so unusual until it totally took Canvas by surprise, and the only way that he knew to respond to him was with a question. "John, what's wrong with you?" Canvas just kind of blew it off, told him that he loved him too, turned and went back into the house.

Now, John was not the type to tell you that he loved you. He was the type that would show you his love rather than tell you he loved you. By this time his sister had arrived home from a concert that the school band had gone to. (Her teacher brought her home.) As she was getting out of the car, John grabbed her and began to tell her the same things – how much he loved her. She told John that she loved him too and kind of kept on walking with her flute and bag in her hand and casually asked me, "Mama, what wrong with John?"

"He's all right," I said, and she went on into the house, tired from a full day. She went to her room to relax.

By this time, John had vented a lot of emotions and he appeared now more at peace after seeing, hugging and telling us all that he loved us. We sat back down on the steps again. Everything was silent for a while. Then he asked the strangest thing, "Mama, where is my Big Daddy?"

I said, "He's in heaven."

Then he asked, "Where is my Grand mama?"

"She's in heaven too."

In a very soft, gentle voice, he said, "I'm going to heaven too."

I said, "Say what? What you said boy?"

He would not repeat it again. No matter how hard I tried to get it out of him, he would not say it again. But it appeared that a greater peace came over him as he finally released what he was really trying to say, (but was having a very hard time trying to accept.) He released a sigh of relief as he took a long, deep breath and held onto me with a such a warm, loving hug that I will never forget. I tried still again to get him to explain to me what he meant about going to heaven.

I said, "Boy I know you're not talking about dying."

He never said a word.

So I asked him, "John, have you accepted Jesus Christ as your Lord and Savior?"

He did not say anything. He just sat there looking up into the sky at the stars.

Then I told him, "Well, I take that to be a no. But would you like to accept Jesus Christ as your Lord and Savior?"

And he said yes. I led him into prayer and he received Christ into his heart. I asked him to spend the night with us and he could sleep in his old room.

"All right," he said. He immediately got up and went to the car where his girlfriend was waiting for him and said good-night to her. After saying goodnight to her, he said goodnight to me, his aunt and my husband and he went straight to his room. My husband went back in to watch TV while my sister and I stayed outside pondering the matter. Before I retired, I peaked in on him, and he looked peaceful lying there asleep. The next morning I was led by the spirit just to stay home and spend it with him and make a big Sunday morning breakfast and dinner.

However, when he got up that Sunday, he did not want any breakfast. I could tell that he was still not quite himself. He did stay with us until lunchtime, then he said that he had to be getting on home. We did not get the chance to share a meal together, but that's not so important. What was important to me was that we got the chance to spend that time together and I thank and praise the Lord for that because exactly 28 days later, John was gone.

Yes, gone to be with the Lord and I do believe that the Lord told him about the plans that he had for his life and that his time here was up. It was time for him to go home. That's the home John kept referring to, but he was not ready to go. He wanted to live a little while longer to fulfill some of the dreams he had – for they were many.

He had set many goals. He had moved out on his own, he'd bought a jeep and a BMW, and was planning to buy himself a new home that Christmas. But, God had a bigger and better plan for John.

That is what I shared with my family that Thanksgiving Day – how John barely made it in. He was only 20 years old. He had his whole life ahead of him. He was very outgoing and he had pretty well established a nice, comfortable life himself when his life came to an abrupt end.

I told my family that we do not know when the Lord will return and we may not get the warning that John had to get our house in order. The Lord just may return at any time unannounced.

After sharing John's testimony, I asked if there was anyone there that had not accepted Jesus Christ as their Lord and Personal Savior. Twenty-eight of my family members gave their lives to the Lord as a result of John's testimony that day. Hallelujah, Glory to God!

I often think back to the words of my former pastor who had said that some good would come out of this. It did – and it still is. Although John is not here to tell his story and to give his account of what happened to him, every chance I get, I tell his testimony so that Jesus may be glorified – and not Satan. My testimony in all of this is that Satan is real. Alone, by ourselves, we are no-match for him but through Christ Jesus who empowers us through the Holy Ghost, we are more than conquerors. We have to know who we are in the Lord and know all of our righteousness, because Satan will come to us in a three piece suit. He does not have horns sticking up out of his head like one might imagine. He will speak to you at a time when you least expect, at your weakest moment. He was the one that announced to me, "Your son is dead, Look what your God have done to him! He killed him." I thank and praise God that I was under a biblical teaching that taught the Word of God and I was in a place in my walk in the Lord that I understood, believed and had faith in God. The other good thing that came out of it was that I had to set the record straight with Satan. So, I called a meeting with the devil. I reminded him who I was in Christ Jesus and who God was.

God is a God of life – and life more abundantly. I told Satan, I knew that he was the one that stole my son's life – not God – because Satan is the thief that comes to steal, kill and destroy. I told him he would pay for what he had tried to do to me, (to get me to turn my back on the Lord by accusing God of killing my son.) His punishment already began just for saying that God killed my son. I had two more children – and God knows that I love them dearly and I would lay down my life for them. But if God required me to release them into his hands (and should he take them home to live with him,) I would gladly and willingly give them both back over to him. As much as it would hurt me, I would do it for his glory.

The third day into the death (and resurrection) of my son, I got up from the chair in which I was sitting and went to my bedroom. I just wanted to be alone with my thoughts, so I thought. Little did I know this was a move ordained by the Holy Ghost. Once I was in my room, I closed the door and laid across the bed. I wanted to ask God *Why?* but I never did. The thought was so strong in my spirit. I just lay there crying, then I heard the bedroom door squeaking, as if someone was entering the room. I never opened my eyes to look around because so many people were in and out of the house, coming and going to pay their respects. I just thought if I laid still with my eyes closed, whoever it was would think that I was asleep and let me be.

I felt the presence of someone being in the room with me, standing nearby. However no one ever said anything. Then I turned, laying on my side toward the door, I opened my eyes and the room was lit up with a glow that was so warm and loving – still I did not see anybody. Then a soft voice spoke out of the light, "Why do you seek the living among the dead? He is not there. He has risen."

Suddenly, in a twinkling of an eye, the room was back to normal. But I was not. For whatever reason, a peace came upon me that is indescribable – and as I lay there, my mind took me back to the book of Matthew, "In the end of the Sabbath, as it began to dawn toward the first day of the week, came Mary Magdalene and the other Mary to see the Sepulcher. And behold, there was a great earthquake for the angel of the Lord descended from heaven and came and rolled back the stone from the door and sat upon it. His countenance was like lightening and his raiment white as snow; And for fear of him, the keepers did shake and became as dead men. And the angel answered and said unto the women, fear not ye; for I know that ye seek Jesus, which was crucified. He is not here; for he is risen, as he said come, see the place where the Lord lay." (Matthew 28:1-6)

It was as if Jesus literally were translated into my very presence there in my bedroom. I sat up on the side of the bed in awe, as his presence lingered in the room. I found so much strength, more than ever before and a peace beyond anyone's imagination. As the word echoed in my mind and totally saturated my spirit, I picked up my Bible that was lying nearby on my nightstand and turned to Luke 24:1-8. I began to read: "Now upon the first day of the week, very early in the morning, they came unto the sepulcher, bringing the spices which they had prepared and certain others with them. And they found the stone rolled away from the sepulcher and they entered in and found not the body of the Lord Jesus. And it came to pass, as they were much perplexed there about, behold, two men stood by them in shining garments. And as they were afraid and bowed down their faces to the earth, they said unto them, why seek ye the living among the dead? He is not here, but is risen: remember how he spoke unto you when he was yet in Galilee, saying the Son of Man must be delivered into the hands of sinful men and be crucified and the third day rise again, and they remembered his words." These scriptures changed my life forever concerning death. I know that someday I will behold my savior's face – and I will see my son again!

When I think of the goodness of the Lord, I rejoice at his eternal mercy. On that warm summer afternoon in August – as I sat in my car with my youngest son waiting for my husband –we bonded as he shared his dreams. That was another good thing that came out of it.

By my husband having his CB radio on, he heard of the accident, which shielded us and kept us from running up on it by telling me to go the other way home. And last but not least, the next week after John's death, we found out that my daughter was pregnant with her first child. And he was another first born male! That gave the family someone else to focus on. Although this baby could never take the place of John, this let us know that God was a God of balance. With the end of John's life came the beginning of Lawyer Antonio Nasir's life, whose middle name is the same as John's. When his little, fragile life entered the world, we were able to focus more on the joy than the pain.

"To everything there is a season. A time to be born, and a time to die. A time to kill and a time to be healed. A time to cry and a time to laugh. A time to grieve and a time to dance. A time for every purpose under the heaven." For me this was another season of brokeness. It was another dream shattered and last but not least, another relationship swerved. Yet in all my frailty, God took my weaknesses and turned them into strengths; He established my growth in him and embodied them into his character for his glory!

Today, I realize that I <u>did</u> get the chance to say good-bye to my son and I <u>did</u> have the opportunity to tell him how much I loved him on that warm summer night when the Holy Spirit led him to my home, where he wept and longed for home. That was what the Lord was doing. He allowed John to say how much he loved each one of us and to say his good-bye as well. Little did we know what the Lord was preparing us for. He was not only allowing John the chance to get his house in order – but also a chance to tell us all good-bye. How great is his mercy, love and kindness towards us. Lord, I thank you!

CHAPTER NINE
"THERE CANNOT BE A RESURRECTION, IF THERE HAS NOT BEEN A DEATH."

"For none of us liveth to himself, and no man dieth to himself." (Romans 14:7)

It was the week before the Passover and the day before the Friday of Jesus' crucifiction. Havoc, total havoc ascended from the bottom of the abyss into our home and ultimately our marriage. That Friday night seemed to be without end. That night, my husband never came home and never called – something that had now become a lifestyle.

"It's Friday night! Let the good times roll," seemed to be his motto. However, there was something different about this night. Something very distinct was in the air, yet God gave me complete peace. At 8 o'clock, Saturday morning, he finally walked through the door; but not to fear, he was only home for about 45 minutes when there was a knock at the door. It was one of his old running partners. He left again without a word. Nightfall came and went, and still no sound of my husband anywhere. At 10:45 a.m. Sunday morning, there was still not a sign of him, nor a word from him.

These things had happened so many times before but I had always prayed and believed God to move in my marriage. I was believing God to save and deliver my husband. That Saturday night as I was praying for him, I felt a release in my spirit towards him. I'd heard a still small voice say unto me, "Don't be content in a bad marriage. Don't be satisfied living this way and become complacent that this is normal. Don't accept this behavior as acceptable behavior."

The very next morning I got up as usual, got dressed and went to church as though nothing had happened and everything was alright. When deep down inside, I was hurting and I wanted to stay home, stay in bed and have myself a good pity party. When I arrived at church, I praised and worshiped the Lord as if all was well. I never told a soul, but I was so distracted. I left my purse and coat in church after the service was over, and I did not miss them until later that afternoon after I had gotten home.

He finally arrived sometime between 11:00 a.m. and 2:00 p.m. that Sunday. He never said that he was sorry or offered any kind of explanation. I realized why he did not apologize:

1) Because he really was not sorry;
2) He really did not care how I felt about the situation;
3) He felt like he had not done anything wrong;
4) I should be glad to see him; and
5) He was sure that this time was like all the other times – that because I was a Christian I would not fuss at him and I would just continue to pray for him.

Despite everything, he seemed to think that I should continue to love him, adore him and please him as the apple of my eye. His words to me, when he finally decided to speak to me were, "When are you going to cook? I'm hungry, fix me something to eat." I was good enough to cook for him but not good enough to be respected or even to say good-evening to.

I am so glad for my salvation and that I walk daily in his commandments and statues. If I did not know that "greater is he that is within me than he that is within the world," I would have totally lost it that day. Talk about steam coming out of my ears! It was all I could do not to explode. Standing there in the middle of havoc, I was still able to hear the voice of God. I heard the Holy Spirit speaking so plainly, "You've still got to love and you've still got to forgive."

I was saying to myself, *But Lord . . .*

He said, "You've still got to stay saved."

I said, "But Lord, just let me have my way for just 30 seconds."

"Are you saved or not?" he asked.

I hurriedly pushed past my husband out the back door to get a breath of fresh air. I said to myself, *That Negro must be out of his rabbit ass mind, asking me to cook!* I was furious!

My flesh will want to act real crazy sometimes but I have to be quick to remind myself what Paul said, "Walk in the Spirit and you shall not fulfill the lust of the flesh." And for the times that I do mess up or miss God, I am quick to repent. I let God take me one step further into his word to the book of Job, chapter eleven, verse twelve, "For vain man would be wise, though man be born like a wild ass' colt." That sewed that up right there.

I wanted the Lord to let me give him one good lick upside his head with my good cast iron frying pan and knock some sense into him. He thought that I was supposed to roll out the red carpet and jump up and down doing cartwheels with joy when he finally made up his mind to come home.

I said, "Lord I just can't do it."

The Lord said, "O.K. let him stand between me and you."

The Lord did not try to urge me, he just told me what he wanted me to know and let me make the choice to be in his will or out of his will. The moment the Lord spoke, my mind immediately went back to my vision of hell. I never want to be separated from the Lord again. The Lord did not have to say another word. I felt like David when he wrote in the book of Psalm 51:11, "Cast me not away from thy presence and take not thy Holy Spirit from me." David was saying, *Lord, whatever you do, please don't take your precious Holy Spirit from me.* That was the last thing that I wanted.

In the midst of all this, another woman was calling me to advise me that, "He is my man!" – and about the affair that they were having. I just quietly hung up the phone and sat down on the side of the bed and said to myself, *Havoc! Total Havoc! O.K. God the ball is in your court. What are you going to play now?*

The Lord did not say anything else that afternoon, however, I determined that I would not allow God to ignore me. All throughout the night, every time that I woke up, I reminded God of his word and his promises to me as a child of God:

1) The battle is not mine, but the Lord's; and
2) He would never leave me nor forsake me.

I reminded him that I was walking upright before him and man, and that I had been faithful to his word. I had kept his commandments and I was a tither and a giver. I was living a clean and holy life. He had promised to bless me and not curse me, to shield and protect me. He promised to rebuke the devourer for my sake and to save my whole house. I would not stop reminding him of his word.

Sometime during that night, God woke me up and told me to read Hebrews 6. I was so excited because somewhere in Hebrews 6 was a word for me in this situation. I could not wait to get up out of the bed to get my Bible to see what the Lord would say to me. I sprang from my bed and got my Bible. I found instructions concerning my situation. This is the interpretation that was given to me by the Holy Spirit of this portion of the scripture: Let us stop going over the same ground again and again. I need to go on with the Lord to other things and become mature in my understanding, as a strong Christian ought to be!

He said that I need not continue to speak further about the foolishness of my husband nor get caught up in his "philosophies about salvation and faith. God said that there is no use in trying to bring back to the Lord my husband who had – at one time – understood the good news and tasted for himself the Holy Spirit. He knew that God spared his life and healed him, yet he still turned against God. My husband was nailing Christ to the cross again by rejecting him, holding him up to mocking, putting him to a public shame. God gave an example in verses seven and eight, "When a farmer's land has had many showers upon it and good crops come up, that land has experienced God's blessing upon it. But if it keeps on having crops of thistles and thorns, the land is considered no good and is ready for condemnation and burning off." Then verses nine through twelve caught my attention. He was once again speaking to me, as he said "Dear friends, even though I am talking like this. I really don't believe that what I am saying applies to you. I am confident you are producing the good fruit that comes along with your salvation, for God is not unfair. How can he forget the way you showed your love for him and still do by helping his children? And we are anxious that you keep right on loving others as long as life lasts, so that you will get your full reward. Then knowing what lies ahead for you, you won't become bored with being a Christian, nor become spiritually dull and indifferent, but you will be anxious to follow the example of those who receive all that God has promised them because of their strong faith and patience." (Hebrew 6:1-12 TLB)

It was then that I got peace, and I realized that what I was fighting was not flesh and blood. This was spiritual warfare and the only way it could be won was in the spirit realm and with love. The Lord began to instruct me as he took me through the scriptures, showing me my way of escape. He told me it was up to me to take it. At that very moment it all fell back upon me. It is funny how we try to back God into a corner and make him deliver us when he had already made a way out for us. He has already paid the price for our deliverance. The choice is ours now if we want to be free. God will never go against our will – not even to save us. He allows us to choose blessings or curses, life or death or heaven or hell.

In John 11:38-44, the writer gives this account of Jesus raising Lazarus from the dead. "Jesus said, Take ye away the stone. And when he thus had spoken, he cried with a loud voice, Lazarus, come forth. And he that was dead came forth, bound hand and foot with grave clothes and his face was bound about with a napkin. Jesus saith unto them, Loose him and let him go." We see Jesus' demonstration of two things:

1) The things that the people was physically able to do, he allowed them to do. He knew that one man in his own strength could not possibly roll the stone away but with the help of the other men working together, they could get the job done; and

2) The part that they could not do, Jesus did for them. In other words, that which we cannot do in the natural or physical realm, Jesus will do it in the supernatural or spiritual realm for us.

As I followed the leading of the spirit, praying with supplication and fasting, I started divorce proceedings. As I began, I faced forces like never before. I was on a forty day fast already, and I ended up breaking the fast for a brief period of time, going on a food binge for a couple of days. I was attacked by a lustful spirit, desiring the pleasures of my husband. The very morning I was scheduled to meet with my attorney, I was so hot and boiling, like I had never been before – but glory to God for his unfailing love, grace and mercy, he kept me that morning. I will never forget it as long as I should live. The Lord had worked it out. My husband had already left the house for work that morning, so I was safe because that spirit only desired my husband.

The Lord kept me and I am still saved! My husband never knew what could have happened had he not gone to work early that morning. Spirits are real and you are not as strong in your flesh as you would like to think you are. Satan will wait on the opportunity to come in, if you allow him because the word of God declares, "When the enemy shall come in like a flood, the Spirit of the Lord shall lift up a standard against him." (Isaiah 59:19) And you can be kept if you want to be kept by God. I can tell you this today – because at no other time have I ever been tried in this area, waking up in a mood to that degree. I know without a doubt that Satan was the one behind the whole thing. But praise the Lord, I passed the test. I thank God and give him the praise for how he kept me and is still keeping me.

As we approached the Friday that Jesus was crucified, it meant more to me than ever before because I suddenly realized that a part of me (my flesh) was being crucified as well. Maybe it was not hanging on a tree (per say) but crucified just the same. That part of my life died. I mourned and groaned in my spirit for our Lord and Savior, while I felt joy and thanksgiving untold that he is yet alive.

As for my husband, I know at the end of us, there will come a new beginning. Just as it was with Jesus hanging on that cross, it was an ending and a new beginning for all the world and things to come that the scripture may be fulfilled.

Early that Sunday morning, the grave could not hold him – Christ rose up, resurrected on that bright and glorious Sunday morning. Though it may have been dark and sad that Friday morning as his spirit returned back to his father – Hallelujah – on that third day, Jesus got up and his glory filled the earth, giving us eternal salvation. An anchor for our souls. I believe that we too will be resurrected back to the fullness of life, restored in the fullness of time.

Three times we appeared before the judge in court, and three times we were sent back. God started a great work in my husband's life. He voluntarily went to a Christian based program for deliverance and healing. He came home a new creation in Christ Jesus but with many challenges ahead of him. I am proud to say that he has met those challenges and he is back on track honoring the Lord with all that he has and telling his testimony of the goodness of the Lord. He loves to tell how the Lord has saved him and how he is restoring him and our marriage, to the glory of God.

Our divorce was dismissed and we have now recommitted ourselves to each other and to our marriage and to God. We both believe what is impossible with man is *just right* for God. What Satan meant for evil, God meant for good. "Wherefore they are no more two, but one flesh. What therefore God has joined together, let no man put asunder." (Matthew 19:6)

www.ingramcontent.com/pod-product-compliance
Lightning Source LLC
Chambersburg PA
CBHW030354290526
45785CB00004B/1752